CRYPTOCURRENCY INVESTING FOR BEGINNERS

DEVELOP THE STRATEGIES, SKILLS AND METHODS
TO ANALYZE THE BITCOIN, ETHEREUM, AND
CRYPTO MARKET TO CREATE A PASSIVE INCOME

JOSEPH REED

© Copyright 2021 - All rights reserved.

It is not legal to reproduce, duplicate, or transmit any part of this document in either electronic means or in printed format. Recording of this publication is strictly prohibited and any storage of this document is not allowed unless with written permission from the publisher except for the use of brief quotations in a book review.

SPECIAL BONUS!

WANT THS BONUS BOOK FOR FREE?

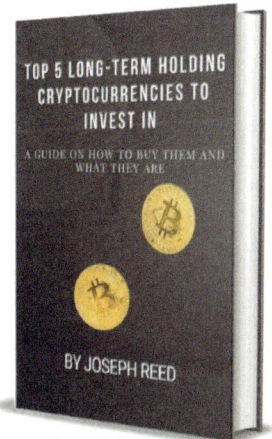

Get FREE, unlimited access to it and all of my new books by joining our community.

SCAN WITH YOUR CAMERA TO JOIN

CONTENTS

Introduction	7
1. FUNDAMENTALS OF CRYPTOCURRENCY	11
How Does Cryptocurrency Trading Solve All These Issues?	12
Transactions and Cryptocurrencies	14
Planning Before Beginning Cryptocurrency Investment	16
Reasons for Investing in Cryptocurrency Business	16
Glossary	25
2. HOW TO INVEST IN CRYPTOCURRENCY	26
Ethereum	26
Bitcoin	27
Litecoin	28
Monero	28
Dash	29
Ripple	29
How to Invest	29
Steps for Investing	32
Basic Investing Principles	33
Glossary	41
3. CRYPTOCURRENCY PRICE, RISK AND TAX	43
The Risks Involved in Investing in Cryptocurrency	45
Glossary	51
4. MANAGING RISK	53
Liquidity Risk and Market Risk Difference	54
Strategically Plan Your Trades	55
Emotional Control in Trading	58
The Common Emotions Experienced by Traders	61
Top Tips and Strategies for Controlling Emotions While Trading	63

Technical Analysis Merits and Demerits	66
Glossary	68
5. THE BASICS OF TECHNICAL ANALYSIS IN CRYPTO	70
How to Read Candlestick Charts	78
Main Figures Of Technical Analysis	88
Patterns Recognition and Understanding	91
Shifting the Trendline for Trend Riding	97
Looking at Good Patterns	100
Glossary	109
6. THE FUTURE OF CRYPTOCURRENCY	111
Success in Cryptocurrency Investing	117
7. CRYPTOCURRENCY MYTHS	126
"It's Not Backed By Gold or Silver—So It's No Good."	126
"Only Criminals Use It."	127
"A Government Agency Controls It."	128
"It Is a Scam."	128
"Cryptocurrencies Can't Be Hacked."	129
"Transactions in Cryptocurrency Are Untraceable."	130
"Merchants Won't Accept Cryptocurrency."	130
Final Words	133
References	137

INTRODUCTION

A cryptocurrency is a digital currency where cryptographic proofs are used for validating transactions instead of trusted third parties. Hundreds of so-called cryptocurrencies are on the market for a purchase, but they really have nothing to do with cryptography. Therefore, they should be called a centralized database and nothing more. Blockchain is the most important subject in the crypto world that allows cryptocurrencies to exist in the first place.

Blockchain is a decentralized ledger system, and if you know how banks work, it's similar to that system. Banks have ledgers, ledgers have accounts, and accounts have balances. But the key difference between the banks and the blockchain is that banks have centralized ledgers while the blockchain is decentralized. Additionally, to make a digital payment with your bank card, it must go through banks where humans would authorize the payments; while the blockchain is decentralized, computers validate transactions using cryptographic proofs instead of humans.

INTRODUCTION

The key to cryptocurrencies are decentralization and cryptographic proofs. In terms of Altcoins, which stands for Alternative Coins or Alternative cryptocurrencies, you need to remember that Bitcoin was the first ever cryptocurrency; therefore, every other cryptocurrency is an Altcoin. Bitcoin Cash, Dash, Monero, Litecoin, and Ethereum are all Alternative cryptocurrencies. Still, many so-called cryptocurrencies out there claim and advertise using blockchain technology. In reality, they only represent a centralized system or centralized database; therefore, they should be called "crypto assets" or rather "tokens." As an introduction to cryptocurrencies, it's valuable to understand how some of the crypto assets work, especially if you are planning to trade or invest in these instruments long term.

Cryptocurrency is virtual money that exists entirely online. One of its selling points is that it cuts out the need for a bank or middleman that will charge a transaction fee or commission. This makes payments, and international payments, quick and costless. If you think of a payment solution like PayPal, cryptocurrency serves a similar purpose: to facilitate financial transactions, except cryptocurrency is the method of payment itself.

The notable difference from paying in traditional ways is that cryptocurrency transactions are not reversible, and they are anonymous. They also do not have the same protection as money that is stored in banks and credit unions does. If you are storing cryptocurrency in an online wallet, and the company goes bankrupt, or your account is hacked, you will simply lose your cryptocurrency.

Unlike a federal government that controls the supply of money, a cryptocurrency is produced by its system at a rate that is defined when the system is created. The individual currency is called a "coin," and all or a portion of it would be used to purchase other items or assets. Just like the market, the value of a coin or a specific cryptocurrency is largely based upon scarcity and supply and demand. Due to the high number of available cryptocurrencies, the overall viability of the individual company and cryptocurrency system can also affect its perceived value.

As of early 2021, Bitcoin was the most valuable cryptocurrency with one Bitcoin being worth 46,000 US dollars. Bitcoin is also the most commonly used currency, although cryptocurrencies are fairly new and have not gained universal acceptance. To date, approximately 36% of small- to medium-size companies in the US accept Bitcoin as a form of payment. In all other cases, intermediaries are needed, such as with the new Bitcoin debit cards. Other popular cryptocurrencies, like Ethereum, are mainly accepted by online companies.

Bitcoin's growth in value has been characterized by a series of bubbles, with the daily value fluctuating up and down by fairly large amounts. However, if you consider that Bitcoin has only existed since 2010, and its starting value was 0.0008 dollars, its ultimate rise in value has been impressive. This may be due to new factors that have caused some investors to look to Bitcoin. Originally, Bitcoin was introduced purely as a digital currency that was outside the control of any one country. Over time, Bitcoin has seen increases in demand and value in times when the traditional market is down. Some investors are starting to treat Bitcoin as though it were gold. Historically, investors have turned to gold when they feel that their currency is unstable. As it stands, cryptocurrency has not gained mainstream acceptance with investors, but perhaps, its use to store value during economic slumps may contribute to its longevity.

INTRODUCTION

You can invest directly in a cryptocurrency by purchasing a coin or a portion of a coin using a trading app. New indirect methods have come about, such as ETFs and index funds. Specific Bitcoin ETFs track the performance of Bitcoin-related companies and cryptocurrency indexes, such as Bitwise 10 that tracks the ten largest cryptocurrency values. Because cryptocurrencies are new and their values have been subject to large rises and dips, investing in cryptocurrency is risky, and like with all risky investments, any potential investor should conduct thorough research before getting into the game.

Cryptocurrency has gained a lot of hype since it hit its climax in 2017. Then, the overall value of bitcoins rose to about 1,318%. The boost was nothing compared to some other digital assets that struck deals of about 36,018%. These figures are funds that stock investors would typically make in a lifetime, which spiked many people's interest in cryptocurrencies. You will get to know the different risks that the crypto business involves and how you can control most of them.

Let's get started!

1

FUNDAMENTALS OF CRYPTOCURRENCY

CRYPTOCURRENCY IS A KIND OF CURRENCY THAT IS SPENT digitally. The typical type of currency can be spent and transferred digitally, too, but cryptocurrencies work differently. To pay for things electronically, or better still, digitally, you might need to wait for the currency to become mainstream. Cryptocurrency remains distinct as it beats other forms of money in the ways listed below:

- Most of the credit card and wire transfer systems have become outdated.
- Middlemen, like banks and brokers, constitute slow and expensive cash transfers.
- Cryptocurrency has contributed immensely to the distribution of finances equally in the world.
- In a typical cash transaction, about three billion people still cannot have access to financial services.

How Does Cryptocurrency Trading Solve All These Issues?

In the normal mode of cash transfers, you'd have to have a bank to make transactions or to withdraw your funds. However, the cryptocurrency business depends more on a technology called blockchain that eradicates the middlemen in the ministry of finances. So, once these middlemen are removed from the equation, the cryptocurrency wouldn't be in anyone's jurisdiction. Instead, it hangs within a network that validates transactions.

Before anyone delves into cryptocurrency, they must understand what money is. What makes money what it is? What is its value? Here, we would look at a few points that would help us study these features.

- For money to remain what it is, it has to be owned by several people. And when we talk about several, we mean a whole lot of people.
- It must be an acceptable means of exchange by those involved in merchandise.
- Society must depend on the value it holds and be convinced that the value wouldn't fall at a later date.

Cryptocurrency is a kind of money that is very easy to transact with. In the past, majorly heaps of gold stones that weren't too easy to carry about were used. Because of this issue of mobility, lighter forms of money were invented—cash and coins. However, cash also has a few restrictions to its use. Now, credit cards have taken the place of most money.

To make a purchase, you could quickly swipe the card across some blinking light, and yes, that's very easy. However, the money that is tied to these cards is controlled by the government. Cryptocurrency offers a lot of solutions to these issues.

To build on the topic of cryptocurrency, we can consider a few other key benefits of the trading system.

- Cryptocurrency helps to fight against corruption: When a lot of power is accorded to a particular entity or group, they have a tendency to misuse it. The problem of total power being awarded to an entity can now be tackled by sharing the power among the blockchain network members.
- It will help the government reduce how much money they print: When the government is faced with real economic issues, they usually would have the central bank print money. This way of solving problems is known as quantitative easing. The method usually results in the government being able to devalue its currency or pay its debt. However, this usually leads to more problems as the value of its currency would drop too low. A currency with a meager value usually causes inflation in the economy. In the end, the citizens would find it difficult to pay for essential services as their cash holds just as much value on paper. Cryptocurrency would no doubt help to solve the issue of extreme money printing.
- With cryptocurrency, everyone has control over their own money: The central bank and the government usually handle actual cash, and at any time, they may notice too many funds or some other suspicious activity, and they could freeze your account. However, with the cryptocurrency trading style, only you can access your money.
- You get to eradicate the middle man: Every time you make a transfer transaction, the middlemen usually gains a portion of it. All blockchain members in a

cryptocurrency trade occur as potential middlemen, but they get compensated differently from those handling fiat money.
- The citizens without access to banks are favored with cryptocurrency trading: This issue of trading is resolved by ensuring that digital commerce is spread around the world. So, as long as a person has a mobile phone, they can make transactions. Unbelievably, it has been discovered that people have more access to phones than they do to banks.

Transactions and Cryptocurrencies

Cryptocurrencies help the process of making transactions quick and much more accessible. However, before you can start tapping from the good benefits, you have to ensure that you brace yourself up with crypto gadgets, discover how you can work with several cryptocurrencies, and also get yourself familiarized with the community of cryptocurrency. A few of these essential things include cryptocurrency wallets and exchanges.

Wallets

Cryptocurrency wallets are designed to help you store any crypto that you buy. This feature holds a lot of similarities with digital services, like Apple Pay and Paypal. However, you should bear in mind that the crypto wallets come with an added level of security. Without a wallet, you wouldn't be able to trade with cryptocurrencies, so you have to ensure that you get one first. The one you get should be secure, including paper or hardware wallets.

Exchanges

Once you have gotten a crypto wallet, you can now begin to make purchases and exchanges. A cryptocurrency exchange service is an online service that allows you to transfer your traditional money when you need to buy bitcoins or have them exchanged or stored. However, you should note that it is considered highly risky to store your cryptocurrencies on an exchange. Once you are finished with a transaction, the best thing to do is move your new digital assets to a personal and safe wallet.

Communities

Finding your way around the cryptocurrency market can be made faster once you get to familiarize yourself with the community around you. The following methods listed below are some of the methods by which you can get involved in the crypto markets:

- **Crypto-related Telegram groups:** Most of the cryptocurrencies have their channels on Telegram. So, if you feel inclined to join any of them, download the application with either your Android or iPhone.
- **Reddit or Bitcoin Talk:** Bitcoin Talk can be accessed via this site — https://bitcointalk.org/, and the Reddit application can be accessed via www.reddit.com. These sites are some of the oldest bitcoin platforms you'd find. To get involved, you can start by signing up or logging in.
- **Trading View chat rooms:** This site can be accessed via www.tradingview.com/ as it is a site where most traders and investors assemble to share their thoughts, questions, and ideas.

- **Invest Diva's Premium Investing Group:** This group can be accessed via https://learn.investdiva.com/join-group. The site is usually not as jam-packed as the others, and you can be sure to get the needed support.

Planning Before Beginning Cryptocurrency Investment

Now, suppose you plan on buying some cryptos to save them up for future purposes. In that case, you could become an active investor or buy your cryptocurrencies more often to ensure that you maximize your profit and revenue. Before any of this maximization can occur, you must first have a set-down plan. These plans still matter even if you just want to delve into the trading business as a one-time thing. Here, we will be looking at a few things that should be considered:

- What to buy.
- When to buy.
- How much to buy.
- When to sell.

Knowing what to buy is the stage where you select the cryptocurrencies that you want to trade with. There are over one-thousand-five-hundred cryptocurrencies globally, and the number won't cease from rising.

Reasons for Investing in Cryptocurrency Business

What do you think Bitcoins or any other coin would do for you?

First, let us talk about investment diversification. There are so many ways by which you can diversify your investments, and they include the usage of various financial assets like stocks, bonds, foreign exchange bills, and so on. When considering areas or genres on which you can diversify your support, you could consider industries like the technology industry, the healthcare industry, or the entertainment industry.

Adding a cryptocurrency investment to your portfolio will help you keep things equal. The equality stems from your ability to allocate your assets by having several investment time frames — short-term and long-term. Also, because of how different the cryptocurrency world is from the traditional world, diversification could help to increase the potential for your cryptocurrency market.

Stocks

When dealing with cryptocurrency, dealing with the stock market will be crucial because you would have access to several opportunities to gain from the profit a company makes. So, once you buy stocks from that company, you practically become one of its owners. And yes, the more stocks you buy, the bigger the profit you make from the company. The negative is that the more the stocks you buy, the more the risks you'll face if the business fails. Even with that, the stock market is still one of the most profitable markets in investment markets.

Most investors today would invest in a company because they like it, while others invest in one because they feel that the net worth will rise one day and consequently fetch them high returns. Some of these stocks work to receive a monthly stipend that is known as a dividend. Dividends are usually incomparable with the total value of a company's stocks when the market is strong.

You might need to take note that investing has a few disadvantages.

Stocks can face several kinds of risks: Even if you manage to strike the best types of stocks, you might still have some risks that you cannot eliminate, and they include the following:

- Business and financial risks.
- Buying power risk.
- Market risk.
- Event risk.
- Foreign series of competition.
- The general state of the economy.

The process of choosing stocks could be quite a hurdle to scale through: You have several stocks from which you can choose, and indeed, being able to see in advance how a particular company will perform is almost impossible. That is because the price one sees today only reflects the company's state at that time or how the market is seeing it.

By investing in a crypto business, though, you may end up being able to cancel out most of the risks. However, one more sinister side is similar to both stock investing and Crypto investments. They both fetch less income than the other kinds of investments.

Bonds

These things are also known as fixed-income securities. They differ from cryptocurrencies and stocks in that they allow you to get loans for a particular period. Then, over such loans, you'd receive a specific amount of interest periodically. That is why the bond securities are known as fixed.

Capital gains are also feasible in bond markets, but the profits are executed differently. The difference is seen in the companies issuing bonds with the promise to pay back a particular amount of money when the bonds mature. Bond prices do not usually increase according to the firm's profits, which is because the costs would rise and fall as the interest rates of the market change.

A similar thing you'd see in Crypto, bonds, and the stock market is that they are usually issued by several companies. Many government agencies also give these bonds to the public. So, if you plan on expanding your bond market, you still may be able to select from a range of safe ones to highly speculative ones. However, in comparison to cryptocurrencies and stocks, bonds are safer and fetch you a higher income.

The only risks you'd be exposed to with this kind of security are tied to the buying power risk, business, financial risk, and liquidity risk. Also, bond securities have call risks or prepayment risks. This type of risk is seen when a bond is called long before it is supposed to mature. You'll need to locate another place to keep your money after the bond issuer calls the bonds.

Forex

This word is the Greek term for the foreign exchange market, which is one of the riskiest trades present today, as it has even more risks attached to it than the cryptocurrency market. Participation in the forex market requires that you buy and sell currencies. When we are talking about currencies, we mean fiat currencies, such as the U.S dollar, euro, the Australian dollar, and other government-issued currencies. Here, you need not necessarily invest in long-term capital gains. Even the most common coins are subject to a lot of volatility throughout the year.

Being an investor in this kind of market generally exposes you to short- to medium-term trading activity between two sets of currencies, so you get to buy the coins in pairs. For example, if you buy the euro versus the dollar pair, the euro could increase in value relative to the U.S. dollar, then you get to make your money. However, once the value of the U.S. dollar rises to a higher point than that of the euro, you end up losing money.

You will also need to take up an entirely different method when approaching the forex market. This is major because you would need to focus on the country's economic state and figures like, its gross domestic product, the rate at which the citizens are unemployed, inflation, interest rates, and several other essential factors.

Now that you know what cryptocurrency is all about, you are probably wondering why you should invest in it at all.

1. Gaining capital appreciation

Capital Appreciation is a term that refers to the rise in the price or value of a cryptocurrency. This term is the reason most investors often desire to partake in cryptocurrency. Most of the bitcoin trade owners usually waited for long periods before they saw any genuine appreciation in their capital. Here, we will look at a little history regarding the appreciation of capital for cryptocurrencies and discuss their growth potentials.

Many of the profits made in the crypto market were primarily because of how the needs were hyped. For example, bitcoin was bought in 2013 as the price neared one thousand dollars for the first time. In no time, the cost raised to three thousand dollars for about two years. The subsequent significant increase was later recorded in January 2017 when the price went past the one-thousand-dollar level.

2. Huge growth potential

Bitcoin and cryptocurrency trading was one of the biggest investment stories in 2017, as there were several records of people becoming millionaires in just a night. The actual issue is that most people, or better still crypto traders, have no idea of what the market is all about, so they don't have ideas about the next price that would hit the market. Most people go along with the noises made in the market, which makes it easy for the costs to fall once the big movers play for their excellence.

In actuality, going in the opposite direction from the market's moves is one key factor that sustains the crypto market. Once you notice that the majority of the market is beginning to panic about a drop in the value of an asset, it's indeed the best time for you to stack upon it. This principle also holds with the crypto market. Once the price bottoms out, you'd see that the value would have nowhere else to go but up.

3. Increasing the income potential

Capital appreciation is one of the beautiful things you want to look out for when investing in your cryptocurrency. You could also want to make good use of cryptocurrencies that pay similar to the dividends offered in a stock market. A dividend, by the way, is a sum of money that public companies use to pay their shareholders regularly. The U.S corporations usually dish out billions in dividends each year, but most investors would prefer capital gains because it is much quicker and can easily supersede dividend payments.

In the traditional stock markets, though, companies pay their dividends once every four months. A board of directors determines whether they pay the shareholders in dividends or not. Sometimes, the directors agree to pay dividends when they see that the stock value isn't doing too well. They choose higher dividend rates to keep the investors' eyes on the stocks. Investors with lower risk tolerances may prefer dividend retributions to capital gains, which is because the payments do not usually fluctuate as much as the value of the stocks does.

4. The basis on crypto dividends

There are two ways with which you can generate a regular income in a crypto market, and they include the following:

- HODL-ing: This term means to hold on for dear life. It is the payment methods that come out similarly to traditional dividends. Some cryptocurrencies pay out the HODL-ers while others simply buy and take the digital coins away in their wallets.
- Proof-of-stake: This term is a light sense of crypto mining. When you stake a coin, it means that you set it aside so that it won't be used in the blockchain network.

Having tons of stakes means that you have a higher chance of getting paid randomly via network links. Annual returns usually vary from one to five percent, all depending on the coin.

5. Fuelling ideological empowerment

Blockchain technology is that tool that keeps the crypto market running. It is the technology that lies beneath most cryptocurrencies, as it can make almost every industry in the world revolutionary. The technology also offers so much as it is directed at resolving several economic and financial problems in the world, starting from dealing with errors of the divided economy to the banking of the unbanked.

6. The economy of the future

We live in a time where the idea of a sharing economy is bursting into ideal topics. The concept allows people to rent out their properties for use by others. Most of the internet spotlights, like Facebook and Twitter, depend on the quotas made by the users to fetch their platforms a lot of value. So, if you have ever taken an Uber, you are a part of the economic sharing crowd. However, even with that, the traditional sharing economy has issues like the ones listed below:

- A lot of money is required for building the platforms.
- The individual users may not benefit from the underlying corporations. In most cases, the value produced by the crows is not typically distributed among those contributed to the production of value. So, all the profits are generally gathered by the intermediary men that handle the platforms.
- Most companies use their power inappropriately by gaining access to private data files without the knowledge of their customers.

To fight these issues, many companies have resolved to develop blockchain sharing economy platforms. These platforms are affordable to use and will offer a lot of transparency. This system will also eliminate the need for intermediaries when making transactions. However, you should note that not all cryptocurrencies are free. Sometimes, you may have to pay fees, like network fees, which are the funds that are to be distributed amongst the blockchain network members who mine your coins. Even with all of these, the blockchain remains one solid pillar behind the future's economy.

7. Freedom from government controlled currency

The rise of bitcoin and the other currencies was enabled without oversight of a central bank guaranteeing market conduct. Most cryptocurrencies will never be subject to money printing by most major banks. These cryptocurrencies work under controlled supply levels, which means that there is little to the printing of money. Most networks restrict the supply of tokens even in situations where the demand is high. All cryptocurrencies will control the supply of the token by schedules written in the code. This means that the money supply of a cryptocurrency in the future can be calculated even today.

The lack of control over cryptocurrencies will also go a long way to reduce the risk of inflation. When a particular government applies bad policies and consequently becomes corrupt, the country's currency suffers a great deal. This fluctuation could end up leading to the government printing out more money.

8. Help for the unbanked and underbanked

This is one of the many issues that can be solved by cryptocurrency trading. Most people live in low- and middle-income emerging markets, then, in high-income countries, many people usually find it hard to use the banks to meet their day-to-day financial needs. This only means that the people do not have access to the convenience, security, and interest that most banks offer.

In the case of being underbanked, there's the issue of many people accessing bank accounts that do not have the proper access to the financial services that banks offer. With the aid of the blockchain technology, cryptocurrencies have now been able to help the underbanked and the unbanked by allowing them the grace to create financial alternatives efficiently and transparently. Mostly, what people need is a mobile phone with which they can use to start using cryptocurrencies.

We have seen what is needed when it comes to the essentials of cryptocurrency in this chapter, from conducting crypto transactions, what you need to do as a planning process, and why you should invest in cryptocurrencies. Next chapter, we will take it further and learn the steps and principles that guide smart investment decisions.

Glossary

Wallets: A cryptocurrency wallet is a hardware device, software application, or service that keeps the public and/or private keys for digital currencies.

Cryptocurrency Exchange: A platform that lets clients exchange cryptocurrencies for other assets, like fiat money or other digital currencies.

Community: In a nutshell, it's a group of people who meet up online to discuss Bitcoin. It's an internet forum where you can talk about anything.

HODL: The term "HODL" is a misspelling of "hold," and it refers to cryptocurrency traders' buy-and-hold strategy.

HODL-ers: Cryptocurrency investors that acquire and keep their holdings regardless of price fluctuations.

Proof-of-stake: A person's capacity to validate or mine block transactions, which is proportionate to the quantity of coins they own.

2

HOW TO INVEST IN CRYPTOCURRENCY

THE WORLD OF CRYPTOCURRENCY IS RAPIDLY GROWING, AND SINCE its conception, Bitcoin has managed to outperform other investments, like gold, stocks, or even real estate. Plenty of new cryptocurrencies have come into existence, and only a handful of these have features that make them different from the rest. These cryptocurrencies are the true outliers—the ones with the power to change or transform the financial and economic sector. In this chapter, you will learn about the best cryptocurrencies that you can invest in. The following cryptocurrencies aren't mentioned in any particular order, and they all make potentially good investments.

Ethereum

A real outlier, the Ethereum platform provides a framework for executing smart contracts that run on a decentralized network. The team managing Ethereum is full of digital wizards, who are good at what they do. Apart from the team, the degree of adoption that Ether enjoys is quite phenomenal as well. A developer can make use of Ethereum for running Dapps (distributed applications), and it is a peer-to-peer network. These computer programs could be made up of anything, and the network has been optimized to carry out rules that will help in the execution of standards mechanically when a couple of conditions have been met, like a contract for instance.

Ethereum makes use of its own decentralized public blockchain mechanism for storing data in a cryptographical manner, executes it, and even protects these contracts. Every computer on this network will download a tiny virtual machine that syncs to the Ethereum blockchain and is available for the execution of different contracts. This diverse network of different computers provides convenience, security, reliability, and the computing prowess that you will need for the implementation of particular arrangements.

This network isn't free or even private, so developers just make use of it for obtaining consensus on outcomes and when their data is publicly available. It doesn't operate the way a digital currency or payment system would, and instead, it aims to provide fuel that will help in the functioning of the Dapps or decentralized applications on the network. This might sound a little complicated, but it isn't. Think of this as a decentralized online notebook for deleting, posting, or modifying a note, and you will be required to pay a transaction fee in the form of Ether to make the necessary changes.

Bitcoin

One of the most popular cryptocurrencies is Bitcoin. Over the last couple of years, this currency has certainly proved its mettle. A Bitcoin is worth more than an ounce of gold at present. The Bitcoin network is quite effective while conducting transactions and provides complete anonymity to the users. It makes use of the blockchain technology for securing the transactions. You will learn more about Bitcoins in the coming chapters.

Litecoin

Charles Lee, a former Google engineer, unveiled Litecoin, which was introduced as the silver to the gold of Bitcoin. Lee came up with the idea of Litecoin to fix the problems that Bitcoins posed. Litecoin doesn't get issued by a government, like other currencies. The government has singularly been the entity throughout history that has been responsible for minting money.

The Federal Reserve doesn't regulate Litecoins, and they aren't minted by a press at the Bureau of Engraving and Printing. A complicated process, referred to as mining, creates Litecoins. This process comprises the processing and verification of several Litecoin transactions.

Unlike fiat currency, the number of Litecoins present has a cap. No more than 84 million Litecoins are in circulation. A block is generated on the Litecoin network every 2.5 minutes. The block is made up of ledger entries of Litecoin transactions that take place around the world. This is where Litecoin derives its value.

The block of transactions is verified by using mining software and is visible to any miner who wishes to see it. Once a block is verified, the next block will enter the chain, and this would contain the record of all the Litecoin transactions ever transacted.

Monero

Monero was created as a more secure alternative to bitcoin, with the main difference being that transactions are completely anonymous and cannot be traced. The network uses a special kind of cryptography called CryptoNote in order to achieve this and is also completely decentralised.

Dash

This network is similar to Bitcoin, but it has been designed specifically for point-of-sale purchases. The cryptocurrency was launched in 2014 by Evan Duffield after he noticed that Bitcoin had some serious limitations when it came to being used as an actual currency. Dash is popular among merchants because of its speed and efficiency when making point-of-sale purchases.

Ripple

This is a relatively new network that was created in 2012 by Chris Larsen and Jed McCaleb. The network is designed to allow for the transfer of any currency, not just cryptocurrencies, and it uses a unique technology called the Ripple Protocol consensus algorithm in order to achieve this. The platform has attracted a lot of attention because it also features fast transaction speeds and can be used to transfer any currency—including pounds, euros, yen, or even US dollars.

It can also be used to transfer any of the hundred-plus currencies that are available on the network. This makes it easy for banks and other financial institutions to use Ripple as an alternative to traditional payment methods, like SWIFT.

How to Invest

One of the most interesting and rewarding ways in which you can grow your capital is by investing in cryptocurrencies. Media has been hailing Bitcoin as the new gold. The growth potential of cryptocurrencies is unparalleled, and they can hold capital in a better manner than the conventional investment instruments. Here are the three simple questions that you should be able to answer before you can start investing in cryptocurrency.

Which cryptocurrency to choose?

Before you decide to invest in Bitcoin, Litecoin, or Ethereum, you should take some time to figure out if cryptocurrency suits your needs. You should be sure of the cryptocurrency that you want to invest in. You will need to do plenty of research on your own to figure out if a currency has the potential of it being used by the public at large. The best thing about a cryptocurrency is that it has a growing community of users.

This will help in making sure that there are plenty of investors for a particular cryptocurrency at all points of time. Thus, you can make sure that the value of your holdings will not fall below zero. Since the invention of the Internet, doing research has become quite easy. With plenty of cryptocurrencies to choose from, select one that will suit your needs. Depending on what you aim to accomplish, the cryptocurrency that you choose would differ.

Which exchange do I use?

The second question you need to answer is about the exchange that you want to make use of. Information about different exchanges along with a list of the most popular exchanges has been provided in this book. Purchasing your cryptocurrency from an exchange that a lot of people seem to be making use of is smart. This makes sure that you aren't being scammed. However, be wary, a lot of people offering to sell their cryptocurrencies for peanuts are nothing more than a scam. To steer clear of such issues, make use of a trusted platform.

Select an exchange that has a good reputation and has several other features that can help you in investing. Some exchanges provide good customer support service, others provide investing tools and guidance, and some provide both. While selecting an exchange, you should also take the costs involved into consideration.

You need to get your value for money. If the deposit and withdrawal costs along with the transactional costs are high, it clearly defeats the purpose of even registering with an exchange. You will need to create an account with most of the exchanges if you are interested in trading.

So, you should consider the time necessary for creating your account. The exchange that you are selecting will also depend on the type of cryptocurrency that you want to invest in. Invest in a trusted exchange with low fees so that you will be able to get value for your money while investing in cryptocurrencies. The platform needs to be secure as well. Since there are plenty of hoax and fake websites, opt for an exchange that has been in business for a while and has been related to cryptocurrencies for a while now.

Which wallet do I use?

You will need to have a cryptocurrency wallet for not just storing your valuable investment but for transacting as well. Make use of the information that has been provided in the previous chapter for selecting a wallet. You can select one of the software or hardware wallets that meets your needs easily.

Using a combination of these two is a good idea. Since you are the only one that's responsible for the safekeeping of your cryptocurrency, you should take all the necessary precautions for making sure that all your cryptocurrency is secure. Depending on your needs, you can select a wallet that fulfills your requirements.

Steps for Investing

Buying your first crypto

There is no time like the present when it comes to starting something new. The first step is to create an account for yourself with a site like Coinbase, Kraken, or anything else that you are comfortable with for converting your funds into cryptocurrencies. You can link up your credit or debit cards, or even your bank account with any such platform for facilitating the transfer of funds.

Every platform has pros and cons that exist, so you should always do plenty of research before trusting a platform. Now that you have made up your mind about the type of cryptocurrency you feel like investing in, select a platform that is best suited for it.

Finalizing a crypto

The number of options available in the market is quite overwhelming, even more so when you are just getting started. For your first few investments, make it a point to invest in cryptocurrencies that are quite popular, like Bitcoin, Ethereum, Litecoin, Dash, or Ripple. It all depends on the kind of cryptocurrency you want to invest in. Most of the cryptocurrencies make use of similar technology for their functioning.

Don't opt for any obscure cryptocurrencies, especially when you are making your first purchase. Don't dive headfirst into the world of cryptocurrency investing. Instead, take small steps and get a feel of what you are investing in. Understand the market and the instruments involved. Don't invest all your money in one go.

Storing your crypto

Once you have figured out the crypto that you want to invest in, the next step is to find an ideal wallet for storing the same. Refer to the previous chapter for more information on crypto wallets. Select a wallet that will meet all your requirements.

Keep researching

You can never have too much knowledge about something. Keep researching and learning about all the new developments that keep taking place in the world of cryptocurrencies. If you have decided to invest in a particular cryptocurrency, make it a point to ensure that you know all the recent changes taking place in it. Refer to different websites and magazines. Read the newspaper to track any recent changes in that particular cryptocurrency and the way in which it would influence your investment.

There are plenty of social media platforms and blogs that you can refer to. Not just that, you can join different communities dedicated to various cryptocurrencies for making sure that you are learning about crypto and allied topics.

Basic Investing Principles

Ideas, opinions, and analysis available everywhere about investing: on the television, Internet, magazines, newspapers, and so on. You cannot get away from it. A successful investor might incorporate other's analysis into their analysis before making a decision. However, the final decision is always based on their research.

Plenty of cryptocurrencies have the potential for a good investment. However, this doesn't mean that you should invest in them. Invest in a cryptocurrency only when you understand how it functions. If you don't, you are setting yourself up for failure. No, you don't have to know all the technical aspects of it; you just need to have an idea about how it functions so that you know if something is going wrong.

Having a diversified portfolio is essential as discussed in chapter one. It helps in spreading the risk. However, too much diversification is a bad thing. It causes the investor to be spread out too thin. A successful investor would have a diverse portfolio so that their risk is distributed optimally but will ensure that it isn't so diverse that their resources are spread too thin.

Media plays an active role in promoting investments these days. Invest in a crypto that is well established and has a good team of developers. Learn more about them as well.

If you don't have well-defined goals, you cannot achieve anything in your life. How will you reach your goals without a well thought out strategy? Luck doesn't play a part when it comes to investing, and it certainly doesn't happen overnight. You will need a good investment strategy. To do that, you will need to determine your aptitude for bearing risk, the funds you will need, the kind of stocks you want to invest in, the portion of your income you would like to invest, and your exit strategy in case the market crashes.

To make sure you get the most out of your experience and to help you truly master the art of trading in cryptocurrency, we are going to discuss some tips that you can use to ensure that you do not make any fatal beginner mistakes and that you protect your assets and maximize the returns you get from your investments from the get-go.

Review these tips before investing. Although it is a fairly simple concept and you can get started relatively easily, it is important that you know as much as you can before you invest any of your cash into these currencies. If you do it right, you are likely to make a great return. Plus, it is always proper investment etiquette to make sure that you effectively research any investment before you actually invest in it. This way, you do not make any uneducated decisions that could result in you losing out on cash!

Buy with funds you do not need

Especially when you are getting started, you should only invest funds that you do not need. If you think you may be able to invest critical funds in a cryptocurrency and hit the jack-pot, think again. Investments, especially in cryptocurrencies, are something that takes time to accumulate and build money. While you may get lucky and make some money in a relatively short period of time, you should not expect that this will happen. Generally, when you invest in cryptocurrencies, you should expect your investment to stay put for a fairly lengthy amount of time. The longer you leave your investment, the better your return on it will be. For that reason, you only want to use money that you do not need.

Research first, buy and trade later

It is imperative that you research cryptocurrency before you buy it. You are off to a great start by reading this book. Now, you have a strong idea of what the most popular forms of cryptocurrency are, how you can acquire them, how you can store them, and how you can trade them, which is important. However, do not stop there.

When you are investing in anything, including cryptocurrencies, invest in them after you have researched them. You do not want to find yourself investing in something that you do not fully understand, only to lose your money because you were not clear on what you were doing. It is important that you spend time researching the exchange network you are going to use, the cryptocurrency form that you want to invest in, and the recent and historical market figures for that particular coin.

A great way to research cryptocurrency comes from basic internet searches, but you should go deeper than that, too, if you want to make an informed decision. Many cryptocurrency forums and groups online will connect you with people who have already been trading in cryptocurrencies. Getting involved in these forums gives you the opportunity to communicate with other traders and helps you find out what your best move is as a beginner. The market is constantly changing and so are the available currencies. For this reason, anything we may be able to recommend to you right now in this book may quickly become invalid. That is why we have not recommended any one specific coin for you to get started with, but rather, we hope to educate you on the most popular coins at the time.

In addition to researching before you trade the first time, make sure you continue to research before every major trade and throughout the duration of your investments. As we just discussed, the market is constantly changing and so are the range of available cryptocurrencies. It could change at any given time with the introduction of a new technology or cryptocurrency, so you want to make sure that you pay attention. The more you research first, the more likely you will make wise, educated investment decisions. This can protect you from making uneducated decisions that could cost you in the long run and can help you get more out of your investments.

Diversify only if you understand

To expand on the importance of researching first, make sure that you only diversify when you understand what you are diversifying into. Some people suggest that you buy a small amount of every cryptocurrency currently available. This is actually a really poor investment choice. Some, you can clearly tell, are not going to pay back very much, and if you were to do some research, you would know that. Some cryptocurrencies are experimental ventures intended for learning about new technology and to see what can be improved. Others are revealed as an opportunity for new developers to get in on the cryptocurrency buzz and are not actually developed that well at all, making them virtually useless to you. There is no sense in wasting your funds on these types of cryptocurrencies when you could simply research them and invest in ones that are more likely to succeed.

Unless circumstances change, do not take profits

Many people feel that you should take the profits of your funds out right away. Of course, this is entirely up to you. Most people will say that you should go ahead and quickly sell, so that you can collect a massive profit. If that is what works for you and that is what you are looking for, by all means, do that. For example, if your income changes and you really need the funds, you can sell them and reap your profits. Otherwise, you may choose to remove your funds and invest elsewhere. You may also choose to remove your initial investment for peace of mind so that you know for sure that no matter what happens, and you are not going to lose your original investment.

Of course, you may have other personal reasons for wanting to remove your profits that may be entirely up to you. However, it is worth noting that the longer they sit, the bigger they grow. Rather than dipping into them, unless absolutely necessary, it may be a better idea to leave them alone and let them continue to accumulate, so one day when you do actually need them, they are available to you.

Cryptocurrency is not for day traders

Many modern traders tend to skim the market on a daily basis. They enter in the morning with low buy-ins and sell in the evening with high payouts. This strategy is completely fine in many marketplaces, but it is not a viable practice in cryptocurrency. When it comes to cryptocurrency, you want to hold it for as long as possible. Rapidly buying and selling your funds can result in you losing out on valuable growth.

If you want to invest in cryptocurrency, you should look to it as a long-term investment instead of something that you can get in and out of in a relatively short period of time. While some people choose to take the profits and make massive returns in a short period of time, the real prize is in letting it sit and grow in value. It is not unheard of for people to buy in with $1,000 and walk out with $80,000.

Buy low, sell high

When it comes to buying low and selling high, this is virtually always true no matter what market you are trading in. So, naturally, it counts for cryptocurrencies as well. However, because of how volatile the cryptocurrency market can be, this may not always be practical. It is hard to predict when the peaks and dips will occur, as cryptocurrencies can often trend on the volatile side at any given time.

Instead of worrying about buying low and selling high, focus on buying low, holding onto the coins as long as you can, and selling when they are high. You may not be able to predict the peaks due to the volatility of the market, so you may want to make sure that you are focused on the long-term gains, not the short-term ones. Trying to predict the market in a short period of time can become stressful, and this may result in you losing out on potentially major gains. Instead, look at the bigger picture and pay attention to it. Look beyond twenty-four-hour time spans and into weeks, months, or years. This makes it much easier to determine where the general market is going and what trading moves you should make, as a result.

Buy now

Many people are worried about when to buy into the market. They are unsure about when the right time is, and they want to make sure that they get the most back. This is completely normal and natural. Obviously, this is likely why you are investing in cryptocurrency: to make a return. However, there is no optimal buy-in time. The longer you wait, the higher the price goes, and the higher your buy-in price will be.

Do not wait for the right time, or try to predict when a valley will come so that you can buy in. Instead, buy in right now with only what you can afford. Thenceforth, focus on buying more once it hits a low point. That makes it much easier for you to actually get started and to not feel quite so intimidated in the world of cryptocurrency. For the first week or two, make it about learning the market. Then, once you have done so, you can start paying attention to pulling the right moves and getting your low buy-ins and high payouts.

Buy the rumor, sell the news

Although this can sometimes result in you not always making the best trades or losing out, it also puts you in the running to stand for a lot of gains. Since the entire idea is to earn as many funds as you possibly can, the more knowledgeable you are, the better. Of course, you do not want to make an uneducated decision, so make sure that the rumors you are listening to are coming from reputable sources. Pay attention to other traders, to media surrounding trades and investments, and other similar sources. As long as the rumor comes from a credible source and many people are talking about the rumor, there is a good chance that it may come true. If you are worried about it not coming true; however, you can always invest a smaller amount.

Practice and get comfortable

The ultimate goal when it comes to trading and investing in cryptocurrencies is that you take your time, practice, and get comfortable. If you practice with uncritical funds, unlikely to impact you heavily should you lose them, any mistakes you make early will be easy to forgive.

Getting started in anything new, especially trades and investments, can be confusing. Early on, you are learning to navigate new software, store your coins, and understand the market. Give yourself some time and practice money to figure it all out, then once it begins to make sense to you, you can start investing more into it. The more you learn to navigate the software, get used to transferring your funds and storing them, and knowing when to buy and when to sell your coins, the easier it becomes. Also, this will give you time to learn how to be patient and accumulate overall market gains, rather than getting antsy and trading too frequently. Once you get used to the entire process, it will be simple for you, and you will likely find that you can generate incredible returns with this form of investment and trading.

Your risk should be managed wisely

Do not invest everything in one trade or coin. Look for a lot of small profits that will accumulate, but do not look for the peak coin movement.

Have a purpose for each trade that you make

This might seem a bit thoughtless, and maybe a bit obvious, but is not the rush of financial gain or trading reason enough? Nevertheless, it is essential to identify why you are beginning the trade, and to recall its idea afterward.

You are ready to start investing, but wait, are there known risks when it comes to crypto investment? What do you need to do when it comes to taxation and making sure that big SAM is not in your case? Let us go further and probe this aspect of price, risk, and tax strategy for crypto investment and regulations governing this investment plan in the next chapter.

Glossary

Dapps (distributed applications): Software programs that are primarily stored and implemented on cloud computing platforms and run on several systems at the same time.

Decentralized public blockchain mechanism: Control and decision-making are transferred from a centralized entity (person, company, or group) to a distributed network.

Protocol Consensus Algorithm: The method under which all peers within the Blockchain system agree on the present state of the public distributed ledger.

Peaks: Patterns that arise as a result of all cryptocurrency price activity, mostly in an upswing way.

Dips: When the price of a cryptocurrency drops, it is called a dip. On a price chart, a dip is visually characterized as a valley.

Buying Low: Entails determining when cryptocurrency assets have reached their lowest point and purchasing the coins in the hopes that they will rise in value.

Selling High: A sell-high strategy is one in which you purchase cryptocurrencies at a low price then sell them at a higher one.

3

CRYPTOCURRENCY PRICE, RISK AND TAX

Before you can invest in cryptocurrency, it is important to understand how its price is determined. As mentioned earlier, cryptocurrencies are not controlled by a central authority. Instead, they are controlled by the people who use them. For example, if a cryptocurrency becomes popular, this leads to more people buying it and using it, which in turn leads to more businesses accepting it as a form of payment. As more people start to use it, the price will go up.

However, the opposite can also happen; if the value of a particular cryptocurrency starts to fall, this means that fewer people are willing to buy or sell it because of its poor performance. This causes the price to go down until people decide that it is no longer worth investing in because there simply isn't enough money in it for them to make any real profit. This is what we call "the pump and dump" effect; you see something pumping up and decide to invest in it, only to discover that it has been pumped up so much that you end up losing more money than you would have if you had bought it at the bottom of the pump.

Before you decide to invest in any cryptocurrency make sure that you understand how its price is determined. Not only will this give you an idea of how much money can be made by investing in it, but it will also help you to avoid losing money if a cryptocurrency suddenly crashes.

First, look at the market capitalization of each one, which can be compared to share price because it is used to determine the value of a company. To discover the market cap of a cryptocurrency, you simply find out how many coins of that type have been mined and multiply it by its price per coin.

For example, at the time of writing this book, Ethereum was worth $2,198.41 USD per coin, Litecoin was worth $154.18 USD per coin, and Bitcoin was worth $35,790.00 USD per coin. The market cap for Ethereum was around $260 billion USD while Litecoin was around $10.53 billion USD and Bitcoin was around $814 billion USD. This shows that Ethereum has much more potential to be profitable in the future than either Litecoin or Bitcoin because it has an extremely low market cap.

The current price per coin, as well as the price per coin for each cryptocurrency in the past, is important because this gives you an idea of how much of a profit you can make by buying that cryptocurrency and when it is best to buy it.

For example, if you bought a certain cryptocurrency when its price was $10 USD then sold it when its price reached $100 USD, your gain would be 1,000%. However, if you bought it at $10 USD then sold it when its price reached only $20 USD, your gain would be 400%. Therefore, the more expensive a certain cryptocurrency is in relation to its past prices, the larger your potential gain will be if you manage to sell that cryptocurrency for more than you bought it for.

The Risks Involved in Investing in Cryptocurrency

While investing in cryptocurrencies can be a profitable venture, it does come with risks. So, you should carefully consider these before deciding whether or not to invest in them.

Volatility

The main risk when you invest in cryptocurrencies is that there is no way to know how much they will be worth in the future. This means that you could invest $1,000 USD today and wake up to find out that it has devalued by a few hundred dollars, or it could go up by $1,000 USD overnight.

This is also the most exciting aspect of investing in cryptocurrency, because even though it is risky, it also has the potential to offer huge gains. For example, Bitcoin was worth less than $10 USD in 2012, but if you had invested $1,000 USD back then, your investment would have been worth over $20 million USD by 2017. This shows how lucrative cryptocurrency can be for investors who are willing to take the risk.

As mentioned above, cryptocurrencies are volatile. This means that they tend to go up and down in value quickly over short periods of time. This isn't ideal for people who are looking to buy in and hold onto a cryptocurrency for the long-term, because if the value drops by hundreds of dollars, it could take weeks or even months before it goes back up again.

Not all cryptocurrencies are going to be successful. In fact, most of them are not going to be successful, so you may want to consider diversifying your investments across multiple cryptocurrencies instead of betting all your money on one single cryptocurrency.

Security risk

Another risk that comes with investing in cryptocurrency is security risk, which means that you run the risk of losing your money if your cryptocurrency exchange is hacked and your funds are stolen. Currently, a number of exchanges allow you to buy and sell various cryptocurrencies, but most of them have been hacked at some point or another due to human error or poor security measures. So, if you choose to invest in cryptocurrencies, it is important to choose a reputable exchange that has been around for a while and has good security measures in place.

Consider that this market is still new. This means that as of right now there still aren't any laws or regulations that govern cryptocurrencies, so if something bad happens to your cryptocurrency, there is a chance that you will not be able to get your money back.

Regulatory risk

Another risk to keep in mind is regulatory risk. So, this means that you run the risk of not being able to use or exchange your cryptocurrencies if a government decides to ban them. One example of this happened in China back in 2017, and it caused the value of Bitcoin to drop by nearly 50%.

Understanding your risk tolerance

Understand your own risk tolerance by determining how much money you are willing to lose before you decide to sell off your assets and walk away.

For example, you have a risk tolerance of $5,000 USD. This means that when the value of a particular cryptocurrency falls by $5,000 USD, you will sell it off and avoid any further losses.

Keep in mind that most people who invest in cryptocurrencies don't have a set loss amount and simply hope that the value will go up again soon, so they can recoup their losses. However, this is not a good idea as it leaves you open to losses that you might not be able to afford. This is called a short-term mindset, and it can be very risky.

Instead, you should always have a set loss amount in mind before you invest in any cryptocurrency. For example, if you have a $10,000 USD limit, this means that you will only buy as much cryptocurrency as you have $10,000 USD to spare. This way no matter what happens you are not liable to lose any more money than you can afford to lose.

People feel differently about risk, and some will not feel comfortable investing in something as volatile as cryptocurrencies. So, if you are new to investing, start with something less risky while you get used to the process of buying and selling an asset.

The regulations to invest in cryptocurrencies

As you can probably tell, cryptocurrencies are heavily regulated in some countries but not in others. If you want to invest in cryptocurrencies, you will need to find out whether or not they are legal where you live.

For example, cryptocurrencies are illegal in Bolivia, Ecuador, and Iceland, while they are legal and regulated in places, like India and Japan. In the United States, for example, cryptocurrencies are regulated in a number of states and not others. This is why it is important to do your research ahead of time and see what the regulations are where you live.

The rules regarding cryptocurrencies vary depending on the country you live in, but there are some things that remain the same wherever you are. So, here are some of the basic rules that apply to cryptocurrency investment regardless of location:

1. You need to be 18 or older to invest

The legal age for financial investment varies from country to country, and it is illegal for anyone under the age of 18 to invest in anything that can affect their future.

2. You need to have a valid identification

You will need a government-issued ID, such as a driver's license, passport, or national identity card. This is required because you will need to have your ID verified for taxation and anti-money laundering purposes.

3. You can't use margin trading to increase your investment

You can't use credit or borrowed money to buy more cryptocurrencies than you could afford if you were buying them with your own money. Cryptocurrency exchanges are not like traditional exchange platforms and often have no regulations in place when it comes to how the funds are managed.

So, if you borrow money from a friend or family member and they don't pay back what they owe, you will not likely get any help from the government or law enforcement agencies.

4. It is illegal to use cryptocurrencies for money laundering purposes

If an individual tries to use them in order to hide their identity or activities from their government, they are breaking the law and could face fines or imprisonment.

Crypto tax strategies

Governments love nothing more than our hard-earned money. Many of you may be realizing your crypto gains this year, and this is going to have implications for your tax bill next year when you could find yourself getting nicely shafted by the taxman. I don't know about you, but I would much prefer that money staying in my pocket instead of it finding its way into the hands of some corporate people in government.

Luckily, you can reduce your crypto tax bill and you can go many places where you'll pay zero taxes on your crypto gains. If you're serious about maximizing your profits, it's time to look at the options available to you as far as tax optimization goes. First, everything in this section is entirely legal. That's because what I will be describing is not tax evasion but tax avoidance. The devil is in the detail, and these are the sorts of details that the rich and powerful are familiar with.

There are plenty of legal ways to avoid paying taxes, but the truth is that they aren't generally worth it unless you make a lot of money. Setting up a shell business in the Caribbean or temporarily migrating to another country, for example, isn't worth it if you're simply looking to save a few thousand dollars in crypto tax. As a result, the first step is to calculate how much money you intend to gain from cryptocurrency in 2021. If it appears that you may make more than a million dollars in crypto this year, I would strongly advise you to consult with a specialist to learn about your alternatives.

If you expect to make less than that, I have some cryptocurrency tax advice for you. First, minimize taxable occurrences. In most jurisdictions, the only crypto-related transaction that is tax-free is the conversion from fiat to cryptocurrency. Almost everything else is a taxable event in the eyes of the tax authorities. Even crypto-to-crypto transactions can be taxed, which is a major hassle when you submit your taxes. You should ideally be holding your crypto and adding to your portfolio with fiat whenever you see appropriate. The only taxable occurrences should be when you convert your cryptocurrency to fiat currency.

This is much easier said than done, and if you're a casual trader, like me, you've probably already done a good amount of crypto-to-crypto transactions, received some staking rewards, been airdropped a few odd tokens, and occasionally bought groceries using a crypto debit card. You can utilize a crypto tax program to help you make sense of the chaos rather than trying to figure it out on your own. Crypto tax software is improving all the time.

Second, consider whether it would be beneficial to materialize any of your winnings in the coming year. Whether or not you can do this depends on how the bull market plays out and which coins or tokens you own, but here's how it works in general. Let's imagine you live in a country where the tax year coincides with the calendar year, from January to December. Assume it's the middle of December 2021.

You've determined that now is a good time to cash out because most of the cryptos you bought in have recently surpassed their all-time highs. Depending on how much money you've made and the tax system where you live, it might be advisable to cash out half of your gains right away and the remainder in the first week of January 2022. This way, you can spread your taxable gains over two years, potentially increasing your profits even if the price of the cryptocurrency you're holding drops a few percentage points over that time. Even better if the price of the cryptos you're planning to sell rises during that period.

So far, we understand crypto currency investments and what it entails. Brace yourself now as we take a deeper look at different strategies, techniques, and ways to handle crypto investments. From here on we will get into details of this investment journey

Glossary

The Pump and Dump: A price-inflating method that uses proposals based on incorrect, misleading, or excessively inflated information.

Money Laundering: The practice of converting huge sums of money earned from criminal activity, such as narcotics trafficking, into legitimate funds.

Crypto Tax Bill: Treated as a commodity, implying that any profits or losses derived from the purchase and sale of bitcoin or other cryptocurrencies are taxable.

Bull and Bear Market: A bull exists in an economy that is growing and where most stocks are losing value, whereas a bear exists in an economy that is decreasing and where most stocks are losing value.

Tax Evasion: The illegal evasion of taxes by corporations, individuals, and trusts.

Tax Avoidance: A strategy for reducing tax burden and increasing after-tax income.

Shell Business: A shell corporation is a company or corporation that simply exists on paper, with no office or personnel, but which may have a passive investments, bank account, or be the registered owner of assets such as intellectual property.

Fiat Money: A currency (a means of exchange) that has been declared legal tender by the government. Fiat money has no intrinsic value and has no utility value.

4

MANAGING RISK

DOING GOOD TECHNICAL ANALYSIS CAN MEAN THE DIFFERENCE between making a 10% or 30% profit. And this is why performing a technical analysis is essential.

At that point you may be thinking:

"If I can profit 10% or 30%, I can also lose that amount!"

It is true. For technical analysis to work, we must be aware of risk management.

In this world, the biggest risk is not taking one. This applies well for life and also in trading. If you are looking for a profit opportunity, there is no better way than trading risky with a proper risk management strategy. We've all heard that trading the market involves a lot of risks, and this is also true. If you have a proper strategy, you can protect yourself against serious losses and increase your profit potential on every trade you execute.

As the cryptocurrency market is highly volatile, commercial leverage requires a more calculated approach. Sometimes, even experienced traders tend to lose their trade. Therefore, if you are a newcomer to crypto leverage trading, you must learn the following tactics for safeguarding your trading earnings.

Liquidity Risk and Market Risk Difference

When the investors in a market decide to liquidate a position or perform a trade, it is called a liquidity risk. This could happen to a bank when it cannot fulfill its collateral obligations or cash flow needs.

Therefore, liquidity in Bitcoin is the average ratio of received or purchased Bitcoins across various platforms.

Market liquidity risk is also called **asset illiquidity.** This entails the impossibility to leave a trade position. This could occur when the owner of a real estate decides to sell it due to bad market scenarios. This risk can help investors handle their investments properly. It will enable them to meet their financial commitments when due.

Market risk is also called systematic risk. A person will likely experience losses due to factors happening to investments and transactions in the monetary markets. This is usually caused by adverse movement of prices. This could be caused by changes in the prices of commodities or stocks. Other reasons include fluctuations in foreign exchanges and changes in interest rates.

Evaluating market risk is based on a principle called value-at-risk. Moreover, any investment decision is bedeviled by this uncertainty.

Types of market risk include currency risk, interest rate risk, country risk, and commodity risk.

Currency risk

Another name for this risk is exchange rate risk. This is the likelihood of a reduction in the value of the returns coming to a trader due to the declining value of a local currency. This risk is considerable if you want to make an international investment.

Interest rate risk

Financial policies made by a government or central bank can lead to fluctuations in interest rates. However, this trend could normalize by controlling the effects of market demands and supply of related goods and services. However, increases in interest rates will lead to a reduction in the price of such equities.

Country risk

These risks include regulatory policies, natural disasters, political instability, and fiscal deficit. On the off chance that you want to undertake an international trade, you should consider these risks.

Commodity risk

Volatility in the prices of commodities, such as food grains, oil, and other household essentials will affect the whole economy. The reason is that such items compliment other sectors of the economy.

Strategically Plan Your Trades

The leverage trading plan is a roadmap on how to conduct a trade systematically and efficiently, considering all the variables that would impact your investment and your goals. A well-researched plan will help you reduce trading risk and define the strategy to drive the trade from start to finish. A detailed trading plan will have an adequate entry and exit point and a clear risk management strategy to prevent significant impacts on trade position.

Usually, the actual market can go against your plan, so when planning, you should make room for improvisation that would help you accommodate the market. If the trade goes against your plan, drop it and plan the next trade. Don't enter any trade without proper planning; it can cost you a lot of money.

Configure Take Profit and Stop Loss

Because the cryptocurrency trading market is so volatile, it's usually a good idea to do some technical analysis and set your Take Profit (TP) and Stop Loss (SL) values before you start trading. TP/SL is an exit technique that allows you to sell your trading position in order to benefit before the market consolidates or to limit losses before they grow. Let's start with a definition of the terms Take Profit and Stop Loss:

What is a Take Profit?

Take Profit is a sort of trading order that is placed in advance to automatically purchase or sell an asset or instrument when the price climbs to a specific profit threshold. When the current market value meets the Take profit value, it is executed. This strategy will assist you in limiting your risk and exiting the market as early as possible at a favorable price.

What is Stop Loss?

Stop Loss is a form of trade order that is created ahead of time to purchase or sell an asset when the current price reaches a predetermined value before being executed. The Stop Loss order is the polar opposite of the Take Profit order. When the price moves against an investor's investment objective, this mechanism will help investors limit their losses in a certain trading position.

Using the risk/reward ratio:

The risk/reward ratio is an objective way for investors to compare trading returns relative to the risk taken to obtain them. This method is performed to understand and plan the type of trade to be carried out, clearly defining the type of risk involved to carry out a trade-in asset or instrument. It's like comparing an expected profit with the capital risk.

In general, more than 1:3 is a good risk-reward, i.e. an investment of $1 USD to make a profit of $3 USD or more is considered a good risk/reward.

Risk management is the secret sauce of those who succeed in trading based on technical analysis. Your priorities should always be as follows, in order of importance:

1. Preserve your starting capital (no losses);
2. Make that investment grow (make a profit).

You should never start a trade with the possibility of losing a significant amount of your starting capital. You should always set a value at which to close the trade to avoid further losses.

Other important tips are:

- Making a partial exit is also a good strategy to lower the risk of a trade that has already gone in your favor;
- If the price went against your trade, don't change your stop-loss, and take the loss before it snowballs negatively;

- Always try to trade from point A to point B, avoid going out of your strategy.

Emotional Control in Trading

It may seem like a secondary issue and not worthy of importance, but that is far from the truth.

Trading is an experience that subjects us to a roller coaster of emotions. It takes a calculating coolness not to be affected by nervousness. It is a popular opinion that for someone to be successful in trading, 25% is linked to technique and 75% to emotion.

The ability to maintain discipline, be patient, let profits run, and cut losses quickly are inherent characteristics of all successful traders.

Easier said than done. That's why you need to have a structured action plan with rules, such as stop-loss, and stick to it. All traders suffer losses, so it is essential to know how to deal with them. The goal is not to lose, but to achieve consistent long-term gains.

How to handle negative emotions in trading?

Are you having problems learning how to handle your emotions in trading? Have you ever found yourself doing something you didn't want to do or made a mistake you wish you could have handled better? If you answered yes, it's a good bet that these pesky emotions have plagued you. And no matter how hard you try, they always seem to get in the way. It's almost like they never want to go away.

The ability to control one's emotions when trading can make all the difference in terms of success or failure. Your mental state has a big influence on the judgments you make, especially if you're new to trading, and maintaining a cool demeanour is crucial for regular trading. Now, we look at the relevance of day trading psychology for both new and veteran traders and some tips on how to trade without being affected by emotions.

The worth of emotional control in trading

Can emotions be considered positive? Is it possible to profit from emotions? I asked a successful trader., and his response was a resounding, "Yes." His reasoning is simple: If you can use emotions to your advantage, you can use them for trading like a pro.

Let's face it. When it comes to trading and making money, emotions can work for or against you. It all depends on which emotions you choose to deal with. You see, some emotions are positive and can help you to succeed in trading.

Those who try to control your behavior rather than allowing you to take charge can cause you to fail. This can kill your trading dreams. These negative emotions make you feel uncomfortable and discouraged to try something new. They cause you to want to quit.

The good news is that these emotions cannot stand against strong, positive emotions. If you decide to trade like this, you will be rewarded. Here is how to win with your emotions.

First, you have to identify the emotions you want to deal with. This might sound simple, but you would be surprised at how many people fall victim to the *emotional soap opera*, the term used to describe any trading strategy where emotions are the main driving force. That strategy is simply trading with emotions...left or right. So, what are the key emotions that can make you a great trader?

The four main emotions are fear, greed, doubt, and hope. Remember that these emotions need to be kept in check if you want to keep them from sabotaging your trading experience.

How exactly do you do that? Well, the answer is simple. First, you must train yourself to think rationally and based on facts instead of emotion. As most other people do, the key to controlling your emotions is identifying the triggers that set off your emotions. Then, you must be able to recognize when you are *off* and what you should do to get yourself back on track. For example, if you start to worry about losing money, you must stop and tell yourself that you will soon get back on track. It is that simple. Emotions are powerful tools, but they can also become your worst enemies if you use them incorrectly.

If you are still a little unsure about how you should react when your emotions get the better of you, ask someone who is an expert in trading or a veteran trader. They will be able to help you get your emotions under control. There are many books and videos out there that will help you learn more about emotional trading. You can also take courses and workshops to educate yourself on the topic further. The important thing is to be aware of what your emotions are telling you and what you should be doing.

Trading is more about controlling your emotions than it is about trading profitably. This is because emotions are the number one obstacle to successful trading. For example, when you are nervous, your heart rate will increase. This will cause you to make decisions that are not based on cold hard facts; decisions could cost you a lot of money if you make the wrong ones. As a result, you could lose money in your trading.

Trading is not a science; it's more like a roller coaster ride where your emotions will decide whether or not you make it to the end of the track. Emotions are great tools when they are needed, but they are terrible weapons when used incorrectly. The only way to control your emotions when you are trading is by being aware. Once you realize that you're getting emotionally involved in every trade you make, step away. You'll soon find that the money doesn't just stop at the end of the day, you can come back to it when you're calm. Emotionally speaking, trading is a risky business, and you need to know when to get off.

The Common Emotions Experienced by Traders

One of the most common emotions experienced by traders is greed and fear. They both occur naturally in all people, but they manifest more clearly for some traders than others. When traders experience these two emotions, they are acting on pure instinct without considering the consequences. They seem to be driven by nothing but their desire to make money. And when this happens, they have no concept of how they get there or where they are going.

Greed

Greed can force a trader to open a position and is the driving force behind most short trades. Short term trading can be very risky if the trader does not have a plan. A trader may be tempted to close a position quickly to increase his profits. While this strategy can result in fast profits, it usually results in disaster because traders tend to become too attached to their winning positions and lose sight of their exit points.

Euphoria

The most common reason traders suffer from these negative emotions is that they set too much expectation on their trades. When a trader expects to see small returns on his or her investment, this often leads to excitement and impatience. This can cause a trader to lose patience and completely miss the opportunity for a profit. Because experienced traders have years of trading experience under their belt, they know exactly what to look for in each situation. As a result, they are not distracted by the emotion of greed, which can easily lead a trader to lose their nerve and quit the trade before making a good decision.

Anxiety

Experienced traders also know that it is important to stay calm when making a trade. Even if a trader is having a bad day, remaining in a good state of mind can help to prevent panic attacks and anxiety. Some think it is necessary for a trader to become depressed before entering a trade, but these fears can cause traders to place too much confidence in a trade, only to lose everything when they realize that they were trying to time the market to make a small profit instead of getting a high return. Therefore, staying calm and collected is important if a trader wants to remain a profitable trader.

Fear

Another one of the most common emotions traders have is fear. This is a natural emotion, but traders often let it get the best of them, resulting in bad decisions. This emotion can be caused by many things, such as not wanting to take any risk, seeing losses as a sign of failure, or being overwhelmed with the amount of information available to a trader. Fear can easily turn into greed when traders start expecting too much from a trade, resulting in them holding onto their money for too long, hoping for a huge return. Fortunately, however, most traders learn how to control their emotions and allow them to keep control of their trading accounts.

Several more emotions can cause traders to make bad decisions, but these are some of the most common. As you continue to develop as a trader, you will learn more about your trading environment and how your emotions affect your decision-making process. As a trader, your success is only as far as your ability to manage your emotions.

Top Tips and Strategies for Controlling Emotions While Trading

Controlling emotions when trading the stock or forex market is one of the top tips and strategies for controlling emotions. Trading the stock or forex market seems to be a place where you can let go of any feeling and control your reactions to what is going on. However, too often, this is not the case. After all, no one wants to make a mistake and lose their hard-earned money.

Develop an effective trading system

To help you overcome any emotional hurdle in trading, you can do several things. One way is by learning to develop an effective trading system. The first thing that most people need to realize is that they cannot control everything. This may sound overly simplistic, but it is true. When it comes to trading, you can easily get sidetracked or distracted, which may affect your success.

When it comes to regulating your emotions when trading, the greatest thing you can do is build a trading technique that allows you to keep things simple. It should only take about half an hour a day to have a system that you can use to monitor your emotions and trade accordingly. There is nothing worse than getting your emotions in a frenzy and completely losing money on a trade. A trading system is a good way to avoid losing any money in any given trade.

Follow a technical analysis system

Another tip is to avoid emotional trading and sticking with a stock or forex market strategy. This means following a technical analysis system, such as a support and resistance strategy. It is important to stick with these two strategies. These technical indicators tell you where a stock or forex may head so you can trade accordingly. However, you do not want to follow them strictly and become overly excited.

Control your emotions while trading by not becoming too concerned about making a ton of money. Emotions are powerful, but they can also get in the way of your ability to make good investing decisions. When you become overly excited in any given situation, you can lose sight of what is important. You need to make sound decisions based on hard numbers rather than emotions. You can use a technical analysis system or a stock or forex market chart to guide you in making these decisions.

Practice with demo accounts and simulators

Another tip for dealing with stress and emotion is to practice your strategy on a stock or forex market simulator. There are some excellent simulators on the market today that can allow you to trade on a virtual platform. This allows you to practice different moves before attempting them on a live trading platform. This can be extremely valuable to evaluate better how the stock or forex market will respond to any given move.

What is not commonly known is that most experienced traders do not control their emotions. Instead, they experience common emotions but are controlled by logic. Logic is a tool that most experienced traders use to decide when is the right time to enter a position and when it is the right time to exit. However, many traders can learn to control their emotions through various methods.

Some of these include:

Taking one step at a time always

Experienced traders will generally only trade small amounts every day. However, when they notice that they are becoming disoriented, they may decide to trade larger amounts of time. This allows them to experience the normal feelings associated with success, such as excitement or joy. Once they identify that they are losing trades, they will stop trading until they recover. Once they recognize the symptoms of being disoriented, they learn to avoid them together.

Reevaluating decisions and taking time to learn and understand

Experienced traders know that no decision is automatically right. After evaluating the data from losses and profits, experienced traders will decide based on objective information. They will look at market trends, indicators, signals, and trends in the markets around the clock. Once they have made their decision, they know it is the right decision based on the objective evidence that is available to them.

Most experienced traders do not wait for market trends to change before making decisions about trades. Instead, they analyze their data around the clock and make decisions based on their experience and intuition. While this may seem like old-fashioned thinking, it has worked well for traders for generations.

Be flexible and liquid always.

The common mistake made by novice traders is that they are inflexible and resist changes to their trading philosophies. Experienced traders know that a trade does not always work out; it adapts and changes with the market. Experienced traders need to understand that when markets are bullish or bearish, traders need to be flexible and not get stuck in their ways. Patience is a valuable asset for traders and can mean the difference between a winning and losing trade.

Controlling your emotions while trading can be difficult, but you can do it. If you want to learn more about handling your emotions while you trade, many great resources are available. Check out some of the resources on the Internet to get started today. Your stock or forex market future can only be as good as the strategies you choose to use to manage them. If you want to stay in control of your investing and not get sidetracked by your emotions, you'll want to know what they are before putting any of your cash on the line.

Technical Analysis Merits and Demerits

Merits

One of the main advantages of this tool is the ability to identify price trend signals in the market. This is a key factor in any trading strategy while trading because investors can develop a successful trade strategy, which aims to locate market entry and exit points.

Another advantage of technical analysis tools is that they are common and easy to use. In fact, they are so common that some believe they have created operating rules that are adhered to.

The more investors use the same indicators to find support and resistance levels, the more buyers and sellers will be interested in the same price ranges, and the patterns will inevitably repeat themselves.

Demerits

One of the main disadvantages of this tool is that there will always be an element of market behavior that is unpredictable. This situation is closely linked to the Random Walk Theory, presented by Louis Bachelier in 1900.

That's why there is no guarantee that a type of analysis is 100% correct. While historical price patterns can give us an idea of the possible price trajectory of an asset, this is no guarantee that this will happen.

In addition, the main components of technical analysis, widely used in everyday work, do not always behave the way they were described in textbooks and publications. As you study technical analysis in more detail, you will learn about standard reversal patterns and trend continuation patterns, etc., and learn what to expect with this or that instrument behavior. But, as you know, there is a significant difference between theory and practice; in life, you will face surprises in the market. For example, if the price breaks down to neck level after the head and shoulders figure, then one should sell. But, this generally accepted rule may not work due to the influence of some external factors, such as trading volume.

Thus, the market does not allow any trader (who has read the textbook and learned the scientific fundamentals) to profitably trade in the financial markets. Difficulties arise when technical analysis is used in daily short-term trading on small market fluctuations, which are mostly just market noise, comparable to radio noise preventing clear reception. Unfortunately, the magnitude of this interference is too great to be overlooked in short-term trade, and it disrupts the market's equilibrium.

To attain the maximum possible level of safety, investors must use a variety of indicators and technical analysis tools, as well as have a risk management strategy in place to safeguard themselves in bad times.

Technical analysis is a tool that offers the advantage of being used in any financial instrument at any time. This allows its application in any area of the financial market. It is precisely this versatility that makes it such a powerful tool.

Use it to adapt to the specific characteristics and behavior of each market. Furthermore, technical analysis can be used on any chart, regardless of the time to be measured. In other words, it can be analyzed in the short, medium, or long term. These features make technical analysis a tool easily adaptable to the needs of financial analysts and traders.

Glossary

Liquidate A Position: Selling stock or bonds and receiving cash is a simple example of liquidating a position.

Asset Illiquidity: The term "illiquid" refers to a stock, bond, or other asset that can't be sold or exchanged for cash without suffering a significant loss in value.

Systematic Risk: Refers to the vulnerability to events that have a large impact on aggregate outcomes, such as broad market returns, entire economy-wide resource holdings, or aggregate income.

The value at risk (VaR) of an investment is a measure of the risk of loss. It calculates how much a collection of investments could lose in a specific time period, such as a day, under regular market conditions.

5

THE BASICS OF TECHNICAL ANALYSIS IN CRYPTO

Technical analysis predicts future price changes based on an analysis of past price changes. It is based on the analysis of price trends, most often charts with different timeframes. In addition, information on trading volumes and other important statistics is used.

A variety of tools and methods are used in technical analysis, but they are all based on one general assumption: by analyzing time series through identifying trends, it is possible to predict price behavior in the future.

Examples of technical analysis include candlestick analysis. Japanese candlesticks are the most common type of price charts on the crypto market today, and the construction and analysis of their combinations can be effective.

Japanese candlestick patterns come in two groups: reversal patterns and trend continuation patterns. The main reversal combinations of Japanese candlesticks are Inverted Hammer, Bullish Engulfing, Hammer, Morning Star, Shooting Star, Bearish Engulfing, and Hanged Man. The main continuation combinations are windows and Tasuki breaks.

In addition, tools, such as indicators and oscillators, are also used. Technical indicators represent a certain averaging of the price parameter, on the basis of which it is possible to predict the trend of price movement in the future. Oscillators, in turn, are used, as a rule, when the price moves within a relatively narrow "market corridor" ("sideways"). Among the most famous and frequently used indicators and oscillators are RSI, MACD, Momentum, Stochastics, and ADX.

The trader conducts technical analysis to determine the best conditions for opening a position in the market, that is, buying and selling stocks.

By studying the behavior of the crypto market as a whole and the dynamics of a specific coin chart, traders usually assume where the quotes will go next. But in practice, often insignificant price fluctuations cannot indicate trends. It requires an analysis of the general situation on the market, the state of affairs of the issuer, as well as experience gained from analyzing the behavior of shares of similar companies in the past.

Because the cryptocurrency market is so volatile, you'll need a trading plan to keep you on track. Many cryptocurrency traders use technical analysis to aid in the development of their strategy. This form of analysis can provide insight into cryptocurrency's past movements, allowing you to forecast where it will go in the future. In an attempt to make a profit from cryptocurrency price fluctuation, crypto traders try to make a prediction to see what the trajectory of the further price movement may be. The set of methods, techniques, and tools used to make this informed and often accurate decision is included in the concept of cryptocurrency market technical analysis.

Purpose of technical analysis

Technical analysis of cryptocurrencies allows you to determine the market's direction as well as the key areas when price movement could change direction. One can use Bitcoin charts to show major horizontal levels, detect short-term and long-term trends, find patterns for entering and exiting trades, and comprehend market reaction to important news.

Diverse approaches and techniques for technical analysis

There are so many crypto traders on Earth—so many ideas about how exactly the analysis of cryptocurrency prices should be done. This situation is easy enough to explain; at the first stages of studying the available methods and techniques, each person selects for himself those that best meet his requirements. Each has its own strengths: Some prefer to work with high probability indicators while others choose to go with the wave analysis (commonly referred to as Elliot wave). It is impossible to say which is more effective.

Everyone comes to this conclusion themselves through practice (it all depends on the knowledge acquired and the level of expertise). However, the most important and unifying factor is psychology—yes, your personal psychology, which has been developed over the years. When you clearly understand what to do in case of profit and what to do in case of drawdown (i.e potential loss), it seems pretty easy before one actually gets into it; stick to your strategy, and that's it, but note, 90% of people fail to make actual money from trading cryptocurrency.

The Fundamental Concepts is what technical analysis is based on.

A few concepts are part of Dow Theory and serve as a foundation for technical analysis.

The basic statements of Dow theory are explained below:

1. The market takes into account everything: The idea suggests that market pricing takes into account all factors. That "everything" includes present, future, and previous demand, laws, market expectations, trader knowledge of the coin, and more. Technical analysts use this information to make predictions about market psychology and cryptocurrency.
2. Price dynamics are not chaotic: Technical analysis is likewise based on the notion that price changes are never random. Rather, these price changes are driven by short- or long-term patterns. When a cryptocurrency follows one trend, it almost always follows that trend rather than goes against it. Traders using technical analysis will attempt to isolate these trends in order to profit.
3. Technical analysis focuses on the price dynamics of an asset over time rather than specific characteristics that influence its movement. Price fluctuations can be influenced by a variety of factors, but technical analysts focus on the impact of supply and demand.
4. Market history repeats itself every time: The psychology of the market is highly predictable, and traders often react in the same way to the same situations. When news of cryptocurrency adoption spreads, for example, digital currency markets often react positively.
5. In general, technical analysis is more concerned with what is occurring than with why it is happening. Instead of worrying about dozens of variables that influence price changes, the focus is on supply and demand.

Chart anatomy

Chart reading is a beautiful thing. I'm not kidding. Not only will charting help you understand any global market when you see the swings and dips on the news, but it's also a direct insight into human emotion and the real-time exchange of capital between market participants. A chart is a historical record of capital flow and group psychology, and in each chart, you can see market moves that made or broke lives. Charts show collective moments of extreme greed, or fear, and offer a means of predicting future movements of price action. Charts are a valuable tool, and becoming a chartist is a skill that often becomes a passion.

What we are looking at when viewing a chart is the value of an asset over time. A technical chart, regardless of whether it's for a crypto, stock, commodity, or any other asset, is defined by its X and Y axes. Always on the X axis is a measurement of time, while on the Y axis is a measurement of value or price. Thus, we are examining value changing over time.

Importantly, a chart is dynamic and must be read as it evolves. A particular disposition of a chart may change as time goes on. Traders should be willing to abandon dispositions if the price action changes course. Charting isn't about proving a pre-existing theory or disposition, although certainly many investors love to charge their bias on an asset using charts. Rather, it's about reading into suggestions on what might come next from a neutral, objective standpoint. You may have a bias, and that's okay as a human being, but as a trader, bias and subjectivity are a danger that can directly interfere with judgment and a successful trade strategy.

Charts are a graphical representation used to organize the information contained in a market. In general, bar charts or line charts are used to show the live flow of a security within a market in the financial and cryptocurrency markets. The reason behind the use of these graphic tools is to synthesize the greatest amount of information in a single box, allowing a better understanding of that information. Charts are often used to make it easier to understand large amounts of data and the relationships between pieces of data.

This is useful in a financial market where asset value information (crypto asset price and others) changes quickly and the data flow is constant.

Indicators

Technical indicators are statistical-based tools for determining future market behavior. These are the four general categories of indicators:

1. **Financial market trend indicators**: These indicators are used to identify financial market trends. This set of indicators is ineffective during market equilibrium (flat) times. The direction of price movement is indicated by trend indicators.

2. **Momentum**: This is an oscillator-type indicator that depicts the progression of an asset's price and the fluctuations it experienced over time. Its purpose is to predict price fluctuations and educate the rate of change. The activity entails calculating the price difference between the current period's finish and the prior days' end.

3. **Time Frame:** When examining a chart, a trader must input the time frame (interval) they wish to see the price portrayed. Technical traders frequently use candlestick charts where price action is shown in a string of red and green candles over a period of time. With each candle representing one unit of the selected time frame.

Some traders only trade higher frame charts represented by four-hour (4H), one-day (1D), or even one-week (1W) candles. Under those settings, price action is delineated in candles that each represent four hours, one day, or one week of trading, respectively. Other traders may look at low time frame candles. For example, a day trader may look at two-hour (2H), one-hour (1H), or 30-minute (30M) candles. A really low time frame scalper may look at a chart minute by minute with 1-minute (1M), 5-minute (5M), 15-minute (15M), and 30-minute (30M) candles. Most importantly, when a trader says they are observing the "daily chart" or "four-hour chart," what they are really saying is they are observing price action with candles delineated in these increments.

What time frame is best depends on what type of trader you are. For my trading strategy, I focus generally on higher frames like 4H and 1D. However, I like to break things into smaller or larger frames for different purposes. As a new trader, I suggest only working trade setups on the 4H and 1D time frames because, as I think you will see, the clearest and most reliable trade signals appear on these larger frames. If you trade on smaller time frames, the signals can become invalidated easily, and the chart disposition changes more frequently. However, no harm will come from messing with all the different time frames and becoming fluent in all of them.

4. Volatility: These indicators look at how market values have changed over a period of time. The greater the volatility, the faster prices fluctuate, and the lower the volatility, the slower prices change. It may be estimated and assessed using past pricing, as well as used to spot trends. It can also show whether a market is overbought or oversold (meaning the price is unusually high or low), as well as trend stagnation or reversal. The

RSI, commonly known as the Relative Strength Index, is an example of a popular indicator in this area.

5. Volume: Utilized to investigate a market's volume allows the evolution of volume to be linked to price fluctuation. When a trader says the word *volume*, what they are talking about is the aggregate number of asset units exchanged between buyers and sellers over a period of time. For example, the amount of Bitcoin bought and sold. In crypto, traders frequently speak of volume in terms of dollars. When someone says, "Bitcoin had a forty-billion-dollar volume today," that means forty billion dollars' worth of Bitcoin was bought and sold that day. On a chart, volume is represented over time in red or green bars. If a bar is green, it means that buyers dominated the exchange of the asset during that period, meaning more buyers were purchasing from sellers' offers than sellers were selling into buyers' bids. Conversely, if the bar is red, it means sellers dominated the exchange during that period by selling into buyers' bids more than buyers were purchasing their offers. When buyers are in control, the price rises. When sellers are in control, the price falls.

Low volume means that not a lot of the asset was exchanged at that price range, and the amount of selling or buying it takes to eat through offers or sink bids is small. *High volume* means that a lot of an asset was exchanged at that price. A trader may say something like "that was a low volume dump," which means the sellers had control and dropped—or dumped—the price, but it wasn't supported by a large exchange of crypto.

Traders often examine volume when determining the strength of a move. Generally, if a significant move up or down comes with high volume, it suggests more power behind the move and vice versa. For instance, a low volume breakout might be viewed skeptically by traders because they may think it's unsustainable and insufficiently supported by buyers.

Volume is also a helpful indicator when looking for tops or bottoms of trends. Often, a top or bottom is accompanied by a large amount of volume exchanged. So, when a trader is trying to determine whether a trend is about to reverse, volume can certainly be a helpful indication.

Moreover, declining volume can indicate that a move (up or down) may be weakening and will not continue. For instance, if sellers dump to a new low and buyers recover the price a bit, but the buy volume is trending down. This may indicate diminishing interest from buyers and their continued ability to push the price further.

6. Logarithmic vs. Linear: When examining a chart, a trader can choose between a logarithmic or linear scale. Because of the extreme volatility of cryptocurrencies, many if not most traders prefer to use the log scale. Simply put, the log scale best balances extreme price action relative to the entire historical record and is particularly useful when measuring large or exponential growth. In crypto, with many assets appreciating 1,000-20,000%, sometimes thousands of percentage points in mere days, using the log scale helps balance and fit the extreme volatility. Log charts scale an axis based on a base number rising by powers (logarithms), while the linear scale always gives equal weight to units on an axis and can over emphasize or awkwardly scale recent market moves.

How to Read Candlestick Charts

A candlestick chart or graph is the most common style of graph used by crypto traders for technical analysis. It may look complicated at first, but once you get the feel of it, it's pretty simple to comprehend.

Candlestick gets its name from the fact that each plot point on the graph resembles a candlestick. They're red (or pink) and green rectangles with a line going out of the top or bottom, similar to a candle's wick. The size and line of the candlestick, as well as the color, reveal important information.

The opening and closing prices of the cryptocurrency for that day are at the top and bottom of the primary rectangle of the candlestick. The opening price is at the bottom and the closing price is at the top, indicating that the coin has increased in value. Green is a positive color because the coin's value has increased. The opening price of the coin is at the top, and the closing price is at the bottom, as shown by red (or pink) candlesticks.

Both ends of the candle can have wicks coming out of it. These are the cryptocurrency's lowest and greatest prices over the same time period. In other words, the wicks indicate how volatile the market is right now.

CANDLESTICK COMPONENTS

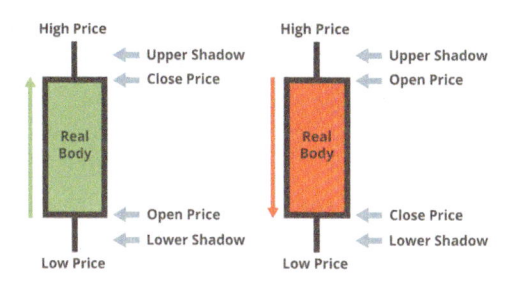

Gaining basic information from candlestick charts

Candlestick charts may be used to see how a coin performed in the past and make predictions for the future. If the wicks are lengthy, this suggests a highly volatile market. As a result, the cryptocurrency has a larger possibility of causing you significant losses or profit throughout the course of the relevant timeframe. Furthermore, given the market's extreme volatility, this may correct itself the next day.

When the wick of the candlestick is short, however, it suggests that the market may be changing. When the top wick is short, the highest price of the cryptocurrency that day was most likely noteworthy in the coin's history. A longer wick at the top shows that the coin was much more expensive at some time during the day before traders profited by selling it. This type of pattern can imply a bearish market, i.e a market is about to fall.

A short wick on the bottom shows that the currency is still being sold. As a result of the increased supply, the price of the cryptocurrency is anticipated to fall even further. A longer wick, on the other hand, suggests that the price has previously dipped and that no further decline is expected. In other words, traders want to acquire cryptocurrency at its lowest price, which they believe is now. This could lead to further gains in the future.

Candle Stick Chart Template
Stock Market

Trendlines

Learning Japanese candlesticks is only one small part of a much greater equation. While individual candles and candlestick formations can give predictive hints about what is to come next, when read in conjunction with the greater price action, the predictive ability strengthens. As candlesticks string together, ebbing and flowing with the price action, highs and lows are created. Traders can analyze these highs and lows using trendlines and can further predict future market movements when these trendlines break or create recurring chart patterns.

What they are and how to use them

Trendlines are one of the first elements of technical analysis that traders should master. Trendlines reflect the direction in which the cryptocurrency is moving, but determining them requires some expertise. This is especially true considering the changing nature of cryptocurrencies. Because of this volatility, technical analysis must identify the underlying trend that is moving up or down among all of the minor highs and lows. Trends can sometimes go sideways, adding to the complexity. A cryptocurrency with a sideways trend has not moved significantly up or down.

The majority of Bitcoin trading and tracking tools will contain built-in trendlines. These can be automated, but you can also draw your own trendlines for a more precise result. Your predictions will be more accurate if the trendline is accurate.

The process for constructing a precise trendline differs depending on the analytical application you're using. In most circumstances, the trendline is drawn directly over the candlestick's lowest price. The line is then roughly extended until it reaches the lowest point of the next candlestick. Make any required modifications to ensure you get the correct lows for both. You should be able to automatically expand the line from there.

The process for drawing a precise trendline differs depending on the analytical application you're using. In most circumstances, the trendline is drawn directly over the candlestick's lowest price. The line is then roughly extended until it reaches the lowest point of the next candlestick. Make any required modifications to ensure you get the correct lows for both. You should be able to automatically expand the line from there.

Bull Market | **Bear Market**

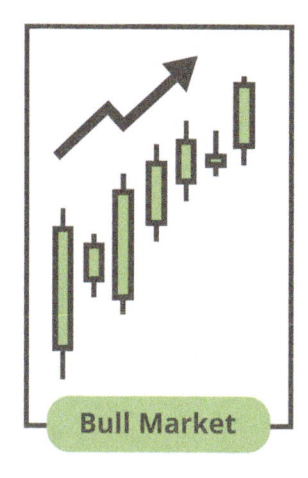

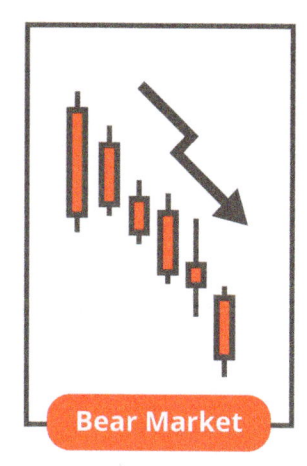

Trendline Formation

As an asset's price rises and falls, it creates a continuous series of highs and lows. A high being the highest price of the asset before sellers take control and drive the price down, and a low being the lowest price of the asset before buyers take control and drive the price back up again. When a new low or new high is created, a trader may analyze the new high or low relative to the previous highs or lows. Often, successive highs or lows follow a general trend of price action and can be connected using a line to create what is called a trendline. Trendlines connect the lows to the lows and the highs to the highs. They follow the overall movement of the market—either an uptrend, downtrend, or consolidation. An uptrend is formed in periods of higher highs and higher lows, while a downtrend is formed in periods of lower highs and lower lows. A period of consolidation may be defined by a largely horizontal period with a narrow range of highs and lows.

Generally, at least three successive highs or lows that touch on the same line create a trendline. As a rule of thumb, the more touches on a particular trendline the more significant it will be if it's breached. However, in some instances, you can draw a potential trendline from two highs or lows and see how it fills in, understanding it may not be very accurate. I find two-touch lines occasionally useful when connecting consecutive highs or lows on large time frames, like 1D or 1W, to see greater trend direction and predict future macro highs or lows.

Whether to draw the trendline by attaching the points of the candle wicks or the bodies is a matter of preference. Some traders have a hard preference and only stick to wicks or bodies, while other traders create trendlines using both—maximizing connections that can be made to a particular line. I prefer to give wicks first preference because they pinpoint the exact price points. Yet, bodies often make more connections and average the trend range nicely. Ultimately, a trendline is merely delineating the upper or lower limit of trending price action, and I see no problem doing it either way. Moreover, a trendline may sometimes have a slight deviation and recovery before continuing to maintain the trend. Thus, an unremarkable deviation. However, a significant and sustained breach of a trendline should be obvious regardless of whether it was drawn using wicks, bodies, or both.

Support and resistance levels

A trendline connecting a series of lows (higher lows or lower lows) creates what is called a support line. Conversely, a trendline connecting a series of highs (higher highs or lower highs) creates what is called a resistance line. The resistance line delineates the upper trend of price action and establishes where the buyers are repeatedly unable to push the price above. Similarly, the support line delineates the lower trend of price action and establishes where the sellers are repeatedly unable to push the price below.

Support and resistance are other important concepts to grasp in technical analysis. These are horizontal lines that you can draw on your trading chart to get a better understanding of the cryptocurrency price movement.

The support level is the price at which traders are willing to buy large amounts of cryptocurrency. In other words, there is a lot of demand because traders believe the coin is undervalued. When the cryptocurrency reaches the support level, there will be a surge in demand, which will usually put a stop to the drop. It can even change the momentum upward in rare circumstances.

The levels of resistance are the exact opposite. In this instance, there is a lot of supply but not a lot of demand. Buyers believe the cryptocurrency is currently overvalued and are hesitant to purchase it. If the price of the cryptocurrency approaches this resistance level, it will encounter an overflow of supply, causing the price to fall.

Cryptocurrency technical experts will occasionally discover variances on this. In these situations, buyers may congregate near the support lines and sellers may sell near the resistance lines. When it comes to lateral movement, this happens more frequently.

A breakout of support or resistance levels in your technical analysis most likely implies that the current trend is strengthening. If the resistance level becomes the support level, the trend is reinforced even more. Remember that a false breakout might happen, in which case the trend will remain unchanged. As a result, technical analysis necessitates the analysis of several figures in order to identify trends.

Polarity

So, what happens when these thresholds are breached?

These barriers finally break once the market has entirely absorbed either the purchasing or selling efforts. When this happens, a substantial shift in sentiment can occur, which is referred to as polarity.

Due to the elimination of sell pressure, when selling behind an established resistance level is fully absorbed, it is no longer considered an optimal location to take profit but rather as a suitable entry point for buyers, turning the resistance level into support.

When the purchasing pressure behind a support level is entirely absorbed, it becomes a resistance level since traders are no longer willing to buy at this price.

It's vital to remember that when price breaks through major support, it's considered a bearish development, which means the asset will most likely continue to decrease until sellers run out of steam. Profit-taking or bargain-hunting triggers a rebound, which creates a new support level.

On the other hand, when a price breaks a resistance, it is considered a bullish sentiment, and the price tends to follow the breakout until the next resistance level is found.

As shown in the image below, when the resistance level was broken, polarity had an impact on the price of ETH/USD. You can see how what was previously a powerful resistance, having rejected price action multiple times, became weaker as it was tested until it couldn't hold prices down any longer.

Due to the substantial shift in market mood, after the barrier was breached, the price soared dramatically. Even after the price movement calmed down, it sank to the previous resistance left, which this time held as support—polarity in action.

Due to the concentration of buying or selling pressure that awaits, price trends are expected to take a breather when they come into touch with support or resistance lines. While the levels can operate as a price barrier for a long time, their effectiveness is limited because the market will eventually absorb their efforts.

When this happens, polarity kicks in, converting support to resistance and vice versa.

To summarize, support and resistance levels assist in identifying areas of high supply and demand. As a result, many traders consider spotting significant supports and resistances to be the most crucial component of trading.

Main Figures Of Technical Analysis

The figure describes a change in the price of a crypto asset that traders detect on the chart on a regular basis.

Head and shoulders pattern

The head and shoulders reversal pattern is quite prevalent after a powerful and long-lasting trend. The figure is made up of three peaks, the largest of which is in the middle (head), while the other two peaks on the sides (shoulders) are lower and nearly equal.

How do you make use of a head and shoulder pattern?

1.Establishing a trend: First and foremost, the establishment of an upward, positive tendency must be stated. This graphical model must be preceded by a significant upward trend.

2.Shoulder on the left: We wait for the left shoulder to form, which appears on the chart as a new maximum with the ensuing correction. Furthermore, the lowest corrective point is almost always above the current trendline.

3.Head: Now, the head will form after the adjustment has been completed. There appears to be strong price momentum in the current trend's direction. It establishes a new high, but the price quickly returns to the point where the momentum began and breaks through the current trendline. This calls into question the bull trend's strength.

4.Shoulder on the right: However, the bulls' power is still adequate to attempt to correct the situation, so they enter the market and push the price higher. However, due to a shortage of potential customers, the price is unable to reach a new high and rolls back, forming the model's right shoulder. In theory, the right and left shoulders should be symmetrical; however, this is not usually the case in practice.

5.The neckline is broken: After the price fails to set a new high, it approaches the so-called neck line, which is held at the left shoulder and head minimum. Depending on the correlation of bulls and bears, the neck can have an upward slope, a level position, or a downward slope. When the price breaks through the neckline, a typical sell signal appears.

6.Profit target: After the price has crossed a distance equivalent to the distance between the maximum of the head and the level of the neck, it is recommended that you exit this trading position. However, this is merely a rough aim that will need to be fine-tuned with other tools like support and resistance lines.

Double bottom or double top

A double bottom is one of the most typical patterns after a significant downtrend, and a double top is one of the most common patterns following an uptrend. The "Double Bottom" figure resembles the "Double Top" figure in appearance. They are identical with the exception that they are mirror images of each other.

The traditional double bottom usually signals at least a little shift in the trend's direction. The junction of the resistance line from the bottom up is considered the key price movement that creates the double bottom.

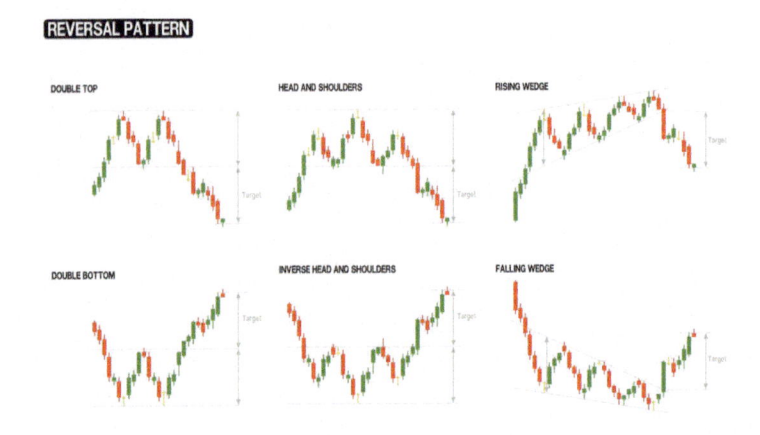

This chapter introduces you to the basics but essentials of technical analysis in trading, Bitcoin and other currencies. Technical analysis works, but alone, it is not enough to achieve success in the cryptocurrency market. You must carefully manage your investment and have discipline.

Having this well-established knowledge base is an excellent starting point for those who want to start the cryptocurrency market.

Patterns Recognition and Understanding

By analyzing the charts, swing traders will always note the different trading instruments that will be close to a resistance or support level. They will utilize patterns such as:

Symmetrical triangle patterns

This is a continuation pattern that has at least two higher highs and lows and two lower lows.

Buyers will push the price in different directions as the sellers. The buyers will keep pushing the price up, making higher highs, and the sellers will equally push the price low making lower highs. This kind of narrowing of the trading range usually means that the buyers and sellers are both losing interest in that price level, and they may feel as though the security or pair is overrated. This explains why the pattern starts wide and begins to narrow toward the end of the pattern. When the trading range begins to narrow when either the buyers or sellers were having a kind of war, it signals the possibility of a big sharp move in either direction depending on who caves first among the buyers and sellers breaking the pattern.

The narrowing also means that there are low volumes of orders in the market at that specific level, since the buyer considers the price level unattractive for them to purchase and the seller feels the price is not that attractive for him to sell either. However, when the price breaks out of this small range, it will move fast in one direction; all we can do as traders is wait prepared for the pattern to break in our predetermined direction of trade and with a stop order in the other direction because we must prepare for the worst even as we hope for the best.

BILATERAL PATTERN

ASCENDING TRIANGLE DESCENDING TRIANGLE SYMMETRICAL TRIANGLE

ASCENDING TRIANGLE DESCENDING TRIANGLE SYMMETRICAL TRIANGLE

Ascending triangle pattern

This is a bullish continuation pattern that must have at least two highs and two lows that can be connected with more than one trendline. The top most trendline will have to be horizontal while the lower trendline has to be diagonal.

The logic behind this continuation pattern is pretty obvious, and I am sure you can already tell what it is. If you thought that the sellers are not going down without a fight and the buyers are still breathing down their necks persistently, you are right. The buyers will push the price higher, making higher lows while the sellers insist on keeping the prices low at the level where the horizontal trendline is. Unfortunately, or fortunately, depending on what your predetermined direction is, the sellers will cave in and admit defeat and stop entering sell orders at the horizontal line since the buyers will counteract that move and push the price back up to the levels where they sold and triggered their stop losses. With this outnumbering of the sellers, the buyers will be in control of the market. After this spiff, the pattern will break, and the trend will resume the trend that had been established by the previous impulsive move.

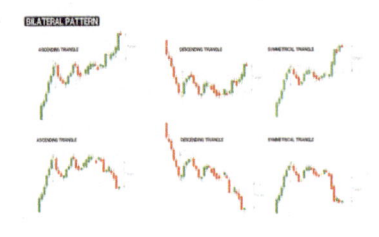

Descending triangle pattern

This is a continuation pattern that is literally the opposite of the ascending triangle pattern. It is a bearish continuation pattern, which means that the trend is down and the price will have to stop for a short period of time in order to consolidate, and this type of move forms a descending triangle pattern before the trend resumes going further down.

The logic behind this particular pattern mirrors the one that is behind ascending triangle patterns. In this case, though, the sellers are in large numbers, and the trend is moving down. The buyers will hold their fort and keep it down at the horizontal trendline. Although this will only last a short period of time before the sellers, who are in the majority, win and break the pattern leading to a resumption of the trend downward.

Price channel

This is a continuation pattern that is made up of two parallel trendlines, which is one above and the other below the price that takes the shape of a channel. This is a continuation pattern that is applicable in both the bullish and bearish markets. The distinction between these two markets is the direction the sloping will occur in. If the channel slopes upward, this is considered a bullish continuation pattern and vice versa if the channel is sloping downward then we can consider this the bearish continuation pattern. Like the rest of the patterns, the trendlines have to be drawn while connecting at least two highs and two lows.

When the trend is up

This means the buyers are in control and the price will stop in order for it to consolidate when they eventually decide to take some of the profits out of the market, but in that specific moment, the sellers will be out of sight. The sellers are weak in this case and lack the strength to correct the trend or even make a minute move against the trend direction. Therefore, the price will just trickle on upward, slowly forming a channel before the buyers eventually resume the strong trend by breaking the already slow-moving pattern and taking the movement further higher. This is the bullish price channel continuation pattern.

When the trend is down

The vice versa of what happens in the bullish price channel continuation pattern will occur here since it is a bearish type of continuation pattern when the trend is moving down. In this case, it means the sellers are in control, and the price will stop in order for it to consolidate when they eventually decide to take some of the profits out of the market, but in that specific moment, the buyers will be out of sight. The buyers, who are weak in this case, will equally lack the strength to correct the trend or even make a minute move against the trend direction; therefore, the price will just trickle on downward slowly, forming a channel before the sellers eventually resume the strong trend by breaking the already slow-moving pattern and taking the movement further lower.

Trendlines

Trendlines are critical components of the trading market. In swing trading, they are essential, as you will see to close and make profits within a specified set of time.

This move of identifying and confirming trends is called moving average. Further, you will need to understand a step called the simple moving average (SMA). Here, you will take all the closing prices for a select number of days and add them up. Then, you will take the total you get and divide it by itself. The answer is the average price of the security exchange. When you do this over several different select days, it gives an idea of what is happening in the market. This idea will help you understand whether putting in your money on a given trend is worth it. When you take the time to understand the market and do your mathematics, the general trend of the market price will provide you with how the market is or has been performing through the selected number of days. If the general movement of the chart points upward, it shows you that the prices of security are going up. If it looks downward over the select period, the prices are going down; trend up and trend down.

To further smoothen how the SMA performs, you can enhance it through the exponential moving average (EMA). The EMA provides trends that give details of more recent data, unlike the SMA, which is broader. To determine the current prices, many traders will go with the EMA as it readily lends itself to helping you calculate the more recent rates in the market.

A(n) then stands for the price of the asset at a given period while (n) represents the period and the total number of periods. As we can see, then, to understand how the market goes, it is vital that you get to know how trends will affect how you trade and whether you will make a profit or not.

To make money off from trend trading, though, you will need to get in early then hold your place until the trend reverses. What this means is that you will need to make a proper assessment that the prices will keep moving in the direction that you want and will not change along the way. Because of this, the risks of trading off the trend is higher, and thus, you will need to be rigorous in your risk assessment. However, the higher risk of trend trade means that you are also likely to make huge profits when it does go right. When you make your move at just the right time and hold out, you will reap significant benefits from it.

Shifting the Trendline for Trend Riding

There are two types of trends in the cryptocurrency market; the first type is the bearish trend, which is seen when the trend has a lot of lower low points on the chart that can be connected with one line and another series of lower highs that can also be connected by a different straight parallel line. The second type of trend is known as a bullish trend where there are a lot of higher-high points on the chart that can be connected with one line and another series of higher lows that can equally be connected with another straight parallel line. It has become difficult to interpret trade in the markets because the process of automatic trading has left the market chaotic and often has prices ranging instead of trending.

The straight line that we draw at the bottom of the lower lows or the top of the higher highs is called a trendline. The strategy to use here is divided into three phases. In the first phase, we should draw a straight line to connect the highest point and the least high point on the chart: this is going to be the main trendline. We then draw a second straight line on the lower lows, and this will be our support. If the prices go lower than the support, you have a potential trend. The support will turn into resistance and naturally, the trader should drag the trendline lower to the right side of the chart. This will make the price action not to close above the main trendline. In the second phase, we draw another trendline that will connect the highest high and the lowest low and watch if the price will close above the resistance or below. If it goes below the resistance but doesn't close above, the trader should consider selling, or going short, before adjusting the main trendline to the new spike. In the third phase, we repeat the first two processes, just as long as the price does not close above the adjusted trendline. The end of the trend will be marked when the market price action closes above the adjusted main trendline.

Using a channel to follow the trend

While channels are perfect for visualizing the trend, it is important to keep in mind that no perfect channel exists on the currency or any other market. The markets are chaotic and break the dynamic support and resistance, but they do not change any channeling component of a trend. A bearish trend will be established when the market breaks its previous higher low, in other words, the support. This breaking of the support will open the gates for different strategies that a trader can apply to follow the trend. One of the strategies, channeling, involves selling on the uppermost edge of the line and buying on the lower trendline in any bearish channel. And although this has proved to be one of the best strategies, traders should look for more strategies, such as breakouts. This strategy employs the Bollinger bands indicator, which gives the impression that price will stay inside two points about 95% of the time. Therefore, traders should be on the lookout for when the price deviates because this means there is an evolution in the trend. It is up to the trader to either go long or short when the trend evolves according to the price direction.

How to make swing trades with trends?

Swing trading is one of the best solid tradings, and it has one of the obvious trends in trading strategies. Beginners need to understand its importance in the market, and once you get to know how to invest your money, it will offer a lot of trading opportunities with a high upside. For a beginner, having enough knowledge about the market is obligatory. The initial step that every beginner should take is to identify the market needs; he should know about the market trends. For getting a good position in the market, every trader should go with the best trends.

One of the most common mistakes that every beginner makes when looking to swing trade within a trend is not entering with the right swing point.

Watch for Counter Trends

A counter-trend is an opposing move that is a part of an overall, larger trend in one direction. For example, a cryptocurrency of a successful and growing tech company is going to spend a lot of time moving upward. As part of that larger upward trend, there will be counter-trends that temporarily move in the opposite direction. Counter trends can represent buying opportunities.

ABCD Patterns

The A-B-C-D chart pattern indicates a breakout to higher price levels. The cryptocurrency rises to an initial high at point A, which is followed by a counter-trend to point B. Price level A represents the breakout price that the trader expects to either represent the high price point or a coming marker for higher prices. Point B is taken as the risk level or new level of support.

After reaching point B, the cryptocurrency will rise a little and show a slower uptrend along with C until it eventually reaches a new high at D. The trader will use point A as the guideline that can determine where to set a limit order to sell and take profits.

Looking at Good Patterns

Look at the charts for the particular cryptocurrency you would like. A lot of different patterns can arise, and the way that they look will determine whether they are a good one to use for your trade or if you should go with another option. When you notice these patterns, you will be better able to predict how the cryptocurrencies that you want to work with will behave in the future and use this to make a profit. Let's look at some of the successful swing trading patterns to look for when getting started.

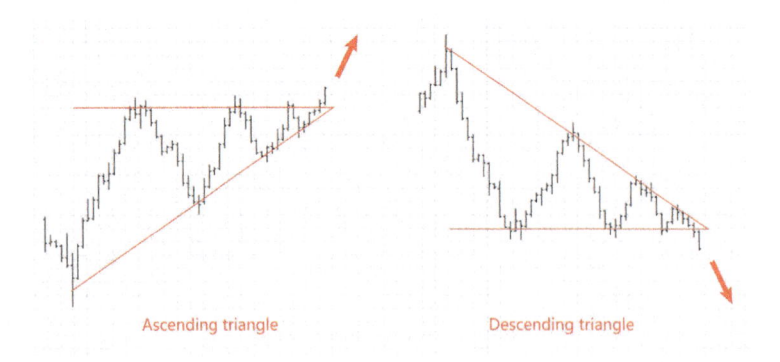

Ascending triangle   Descending triangle

Triangle

The triangle shape is a successful pattern to look for, and if you see it in one of your cryptocurrencies, you will be likely to see success. With the triangle pattern, you will notice that the trend is going either upward or downward, but the variations are getting smaller between the highs and the lows. When this starts to get together on the right side of the triangle, you can see that a breakthrough trend is about to happen. If you see a triangle that goes in the opposite way, it means that the trend is about to go down, and you should not join in.

Triple top

Double/Triple Top

Double top is another pattern that many swing traders look at because it can be really successful. This pattern is one that you want with swing trading. The same pattern works, even if it is turned around. For example, if you notice that this trend is upside down, you can use this information to help with your cryptocurrency.

Channel Pattern

This is a great pattern, even though it is not always as successful as some of the others. You will find this one repeating through various instruments that you may be moving. There are two ways that you can trade for this pattern. One is on the channel, and the other is to trade when there is a breakout. It often depends on which way you would like to trade with your swing trade and how the market is doing.

Breakouts and Breakdowns

A breakout occurs when buyers push the price of an asset above the resistance line. This shows the buyers thrusting the price beyond the general trend of price action, which suggests a shift in trend or a volatile move. For instance, in a downtrend with three or more consecutive highs, each lower than the last, buyers force a breakout disrupting the trend of lower highs. This suggests the downtrend may be broken and a positive reversal is imminent. If a resistance line is breached in an uptrend or consolidation period, it may signal a new accelerating move upward.

A breakdown occurs when sellers push the price of an asset below the support line. This shows sellers pushing the price below the general trend of price action and also suggests a shift in trend. For example, in an uptrend with three or more consecutive higher lows, the sellers push the price below the third higher low, which breaks below the support line. This suggests the uptrend supported by higher lows is broken, and a reversal may be occurring. Additionally, in a downtrend or consolidation period, if a support line is breached it may mark a new accelerating downward move of the asset. Importantly, I use the term breakdown in this handbook because it's easy to differentiate support and resistance breaks. Breakouts are always upward moves and breakdowns being downward. Many traders will use the term breakout interchangeably for both cases.

Breakouts and breakdowns are often an opportunity for a trader and indicate an entry or exit. In the case of a breakout, a trader may buy or long an asset, hoping to get an entry at the first indication of positive trend reversal or bullish continuation. Conversely, upon breakdown, a trader may sell a position to preserve profit or enter a short and profit from the first indication of negative trend reversal or a continuation downward. Frequently upon initial breakout or breakdown, assets revisit, or retest, the point of the breakout, which some traders use as an entry point.

Finally, a broken resistance line can turn into a support line and vice versa. Sometimes, when an asset breaks a resistance or support line, and the price returns to the trendline, what once was resistance may then act as support. A trader may say something like, "resistance has flipped to support" or "support has flipped to resistance." This trendline switch may be observed shortly after the initial breakout or days, weeks, or even months later. If a trendline was respected for many weeks or months before breaking, traders may place greater significance on the line if price action reverses course and approaches or retests it.

Fakeouts

A fakeout refers to a false breakout or breakdown where the resistance or support line is briefly breached before the asset reverses back below or above the trendline. Fakeouts are the misery of the breakout trader. In some instances, fakeouts result in a strong rejection and can lead to a powerful move in the opposite direction. For example, if a breakout occurs and rejects the higher high, short sellers may pile in and quickly drive the asset's price down. Or if a breakdown occurs and fails, quickly bouncing back above the support line, buyers may jump in and quickly drive the price higher. Fakeouts can develop quickly and be composed of a single candle, or they may develop over a short period of time following a trend break and encompass a group of succeeding candles. Generally, fakeouts indicate weakening power on the side that failed to sustain the price beyond the trendline. You may hear traders use terms like *bear trap* or *bull trap*, which means an instance where overeager bears or bulls are fooled into taking a bad position. This is frequently applied to fakeouts.

Relative Strength Index (RSI)

We have said that every trader uses, in his daily operations, a series of tools that help him to analyze the chart he is reading. These instruments can be divided into two broad categories: indicators, which freely replicate the price trend on the chart, and oscillators, which move in a predetermined range of values. These tools often give us clear signals of what is happening to the price, and their correct interpretation is often what makes the difference between loss and profit.

The trading signals do not only come from reading the data we get from the indicators and oscillators, but also directly through the price chart by plotting ourselves the levels that represent the supports and resistances. Since for each currency pair on which we operate we can change the unit of time (represented graphically by the candles,) we have a multiplicity of different signals depending on how we set the time frame. For example, if we are trading on the BTC-ETH pair, we are spending BTC to buy ETH.

Regardless of the modality we use to obtain the trading signal, we must always start from the assumption that the signal is all the more solid the more the TF is set in an expanded manner; a chart with a one-week time frame, therefore, offers more solid signals than a chart with a one-hour time frame.

If I wanted to buy ETH spending BTC, I would wait for a moment when a trading signal appears on the 1W chart, start observing the lower TF, then slowly narrow down the TF to find the optimal time to buy. To reduce the risk, therefore, we never rely on a single trading signal, but we go in search of what is called convergence of signals. If it is true that many clues do not prove, it is also true that the more clues you have, the higher the chances of winning your bet. Because this is what we are doing, we are betting that the price will go up. Among all the tools used by traders, is there one that is simple to understand and that is commonly used and appreciated by the majority of the community? Yes, it's called RSI.

It is an oscillator that moves continuously between a minimum (equal to zero) and a maximum (equal to 100) invented by John Welles Wilder, who illustrated its operation to the public in 1979 with the book "New Concepts in Technical Trading System" and whose purpose is to help the trader identify the points where the strength of the trend is running out; the mathematical formula would help us understand why certain indications are obtained from the RSI. In any case, this does not change the operation, so let's just say that the RSI, moving between a minimum of zero and a maximum of one hundred, reaches two bands in which the trader's attention increases: the 0-30 band, which is defined as oversold, and the 70-100 band, which is defined as overbought.

When the RSI crosses the oversold and overbought ranges, it means that the market is in a phase of excess, in which traders are essentially stubborn to sell and buy beyond reasonable expectations. Unfortunately, to make a profit, rushing in to buy in the oversold ranges and sell in the overbought ranges, based on the strength of the current trend is not enough. The RSI can remain in extreme conditions (oversold or overbought) for long periods of time.

There are particular moments, however, in which anomalies are produced on the RSI if we compare the trend of the oscillator with what we read on the price chart. For example, when we see the price mark a low of $20, rise up to $23, then return to mark a new low of $17, what we can clearly read on the price chart is that by combining the two lows we obtain a descending line. In certain circumstances, however, it happens that in conjunction with the two lows on the price chart, the RSI marks two peaks that, once joined, form an ascending line, which moves upward.

This kind of anomaly is called divergence and is formed not only on the RSI but also on other types of oscillators and indicators (always in the same way.) There are basically two types of divergences: the bullish ones, which can be read by drawing a line that connects the minimum peaks, and the bearish ones, which can be read by drawing a line that connects the maximum peaks.

Any kind of divergence we notice between what we read on the price chart and what is expressed by the oscillator gives us a trading signal. If we notice a divergence in the maximum peaks in a bull market, we have a sell signal. There is, therefore, the possibility of a trend reversal. If instead it is produced by combining the minimum peaks, we have a buy signal.

More technically, we should distinguish the actual divergences —two increasing peaks in the direction of the trend on the price chart in conjunction with two peaks in the opposite direction to that of the trend traced by the oscillator—from the hidden ones in which the logic is reversed so that the peaks expressed by the price are in the opposite direction to that of the trend, while the oscillator behaves in the opposite way. In the following graph, however, we will analyze only the classic divergences, while we will deal better with hidden divergences in the paragraph dedicated to MACD. The RSI, in principle, offers us the best trading signals through the divergences that occur in the vicinity of the oversold and overbought ranges; such signals are more solid when they emerge on larger TFs.

A bullish divergence, for example, built on a chart with a one-week TF in a strong oversold situation and near solid support is almost always a good time to open a long position. The more signals we have that push us to buy, the more naturally we will be prepared to open a position. To simplify, we graphically illustrate the functioning of two classic divergence below (the first bullish and the second bearish); what we see in the green box is that the price on the chart marks three new consecutive lows while the RSI at those lows is rising (all of this is graphically expressed by the red line.)

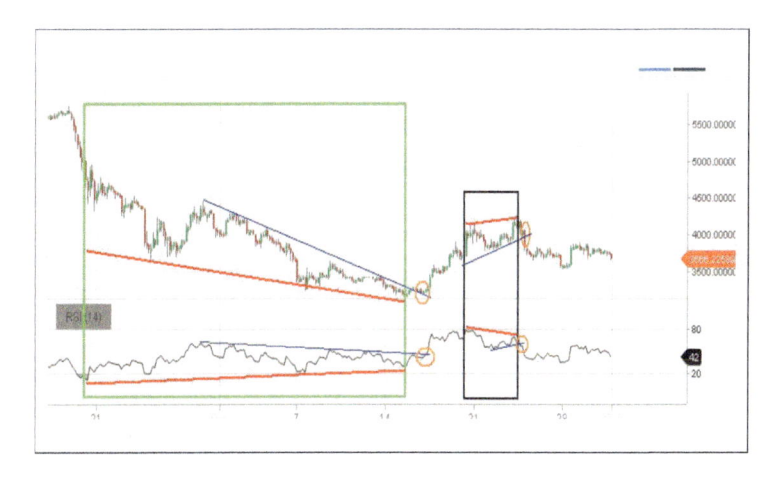

As soon as the price breaks, the resistance begins to grow and undergo an increase of about 30%. Immediately after, however, we notice that a bearish divergence is formed in the black box. On the chart, the price marks two new highs, but the line that joins the respective peaks on the RSI (highlighted in red) is clearly descending.

This time, the support is broken and the price starts to fall. In a trader's operations, the orange circles represent the moment in which it would have been advisable to open the position (the first two) and close it (the last two) to optimize profit and reduce any risks. This type of strategy is not infallible, so by working exclusively with the divergences produced by the RSI, we will inevitably end up in some bad situations.

Glossary

Inverted hammer is a candlestick shape that occurs after a downtrend and is often interpreted as a trend reversal indication.

Bullish Engulfing Pattern is formed when a little black candlestick is followed by a massive white candlestick the next day, the body of which totally overlaps or engulfs the body of the previous day's candlestick.

Morning Star is a candlestick chart pattern that technical analysts use to anticipate or predict price action of an asset, derivative, or currency over a short period of time.

Shooting star is seen as a form of reversal pattern in technical analysis, indicating a price decline.

Bearish Engulfing Pattern is a chart pattern that indicates lower prices are on the way.

Hanged Man: In an uptrend of price charts of financial assets, a hanging man is a form of bearish reverse design made up of only one candle. The candlestick has a long bottom wick and a short body at the top with little or no higher wick.

An oscillator is a technical analysis tool that creates low and high bands between two extreme values before constructing a trend indicator that varies within these bounds.

Dow theory is a type of technical analysis that contains some characteristics of sector rotation.

A simple moving average (SMA) is an arithmetic movement average computed by multiplying recent prices by the number of periods in the computation average.

An exponential moving average (EMA) is a sort of movement average that gives the most recent data points more weight and relevance.

6

THE FUTURE OF CRYPTOCURRENCY

Capital markets

INTEREST IN BLOCKCHAIN TECHNOLOGY HAS ALREADY BEEN expanding for several years in this sector of the market, with interest in the field doubling yearly for the past three years. This is largely due to the fact that most of the changes to this sector have come in the form of front office technology, leaving the back and middle office to get along in more or less the same way they have for the past few decades. This, in turn, creates situations where an asset is bought or sold instantaneously, then it needs to sit around for several days before the paperwork catches up and makes it official.

The Linux foundation is already hard at work to fix this problem and is working to bring together blockchain technology and capital market companies through standardizing a variation of the blockchain technology that will support the existing capital market infrastructure as much as possible. Ideally, this will result in a scenario where a majority of the remaining inefficiency is removed from the system.

As an added bonus, it will also make it possible for those in the field to offer new ways of providing services to clients while also allowing regulators to determine improved means of optimizing settlement and execution times. This will also come along with an increase in transparency that was previously not only unheard of but impossible. Much of this will come about as a natural result of the way that smart contracts can work to improve efficacy across all levels of the process.

Banking

When it comes to the future of the potential for blockchain banking, we should take a quick look at China, who in 2017, announced that they were in the process of testing their own form of cryptocurrency in transactions between the People's Bank and other commercial alternatives. While many of the details regarding this new cryptocurrency remain unclear, the information that is available indicates that it is likely to be rolled out alongside the renminbi, though a firm timetable is still unknown.

This launch will mark a huge step forward toward the legitimacy of blockchain technology and will truly show that cryptocurrency is on its way to being mainstream. It will also likely do wonders for the renminbi as users will be able to purchase it anywhere in the world and have all the benefits of any other traditional fiat currency while also taking advantage of everything that makes cryptocurrency in its current form so useful. It will also help to serve as an interesting proof of concept for national cryptocurrency as a whole because the challenges that Chinese banks will face will have to eventually be overcome by banks everywhere.

China will also see many unique benefits, starting with the fact that their cryptocurrency will allow economists previously unimagined access to the financial data of the country at an extremely granular level. Just what this level of detailed financial data will reveal is still anyone's guess. Even better, the ease of use of a cryptocurrency means that this will mark the first time that millions of Chinese citizens will have an analog for the types of banking services that much of the world takes for granted.

Digital transactions

With the prevalence of digital transactions increasingly used each day, blockchain technology is soon going to test the core values it originally promoted. Specifically, the US Federal Reserve is in the midst of designing its own cryptocurrency, internally being referred to as Fedcoin. The Federal Reserve has already held numerous closed-door meetings with members of the blockchain committee, some of which have been overseen by the chairperson of the Federal Reserve herself.

If instituted in the most likely way, Fedcoin will serve to solve the problems that the US government has had with cryptocurrency for the better part of a decade, specifically that it is an obvious outlet for those who look to engage in illegal activities online and aren't keen to leave a trace of their activities. This, in turn, means that when it is finally offered to users, it will be at the rate of one-to-one coins to dollars.

Things start to get complicated, from an ideological level, because by creating its own cryptocurrency, the US government would then have the ability to alter a blockchain once a block has been verified, which essentially goes against one of the core tenets of blockchain technology as a whole. Adding this ability to a blockchain will also serve to call its overall legitimacy into question, hurting users' ability to trust it and other similar blockchains as a result; just what the result of this lack of trust will turn out to be remains to be seen.

In general, the Fedcoin blockchain will work the same way as any other blockchain, aside from the major obvious difference. Additionally, it will remove all anonymity from the blockchain, demolishing another long-held tenent of the technology as well. This will also likely have the effect of putting the use of paper money on a ticking clock as Fedcoin will be easier to track than traditional money. The public reception to the rollout of this currency will determine a lot about the way that blockchain technology will be used for digital transactions in the future.

Real estate

Real estate transactions have a well-earned reputation for being extremely tedious and painstaking to undertake, in large part due to the fact that the industry has experienced little innovation since the advent of the internet. Blockchain technology is well suited to bringing the industry into the twenty-first century, starting with the listing process. With the right smart contract, as soon as a property hits the listing service blockchain could mean automatically sending to those who are searching for a property that meets its qualifications. Once it becomes commonplace, it could practically remove property agents and listing services from the equation entirely.

Instead, buyers, sellers, firms, and agents will all be able to interact in one blockchain on an even playing field where anyone will be able to both list or complete real estate transactions around the world without worrying about any third party obfuscating the process. Assuming this platform is built on the Ethereum platform, or another blockchain that promotes application use, it will also allow for a virtually endless number of apps that will be able to take advantage of the properties that such a platform provides.

As an added bonus, getting rid of the traditional centralized structure will free those on all rungs of the real estate profession to experience a far greater range of fees than those visible on the market today as they will have far more control of the fees that make sense on a personal level. The only fees that will be associated with listing on the blockchain will be the ones that come along with verification services and keeping the blockchain up and running. At the same time, it will ensure that buyers have easy access to the latest listings without jumping through too many hoops while also making sure that individual sellers have access to the greatest number of interested buyers possible.

Public services

The myriad of individual organizations that make up the public service sector is enough to make the entire industry a labyrinthine mix of rules and regulations that often makes it difficult for those in charge of providing services to actually go ahead and provide those services. This is largely because there is frequently no good way for different departments to share their data. This process is often only exacerbated as department budgets are slashed and the way that services are provided or the services themselves are always being shuffled about.

As blockchain technology grows more mainstream, it becomes more and more likely that it will be used to address these types of inefficiencies directly. When properly given the chance, blockchain technology will competently serve as an official registry for numerous different types of things that may require a government license to look at officially. It will also come in handy when it comes to coordinating and streamlining the purchasing process for a wide variety of products, ensuring that each government dollar stretches to the absolute limit. Across the board, it is also sure to improve response times while also reducing the risk of fraud and errors, while at the same time improving productivity and efficiency across virtually all levels of the bureaucracy. As a general rule, wherever governmental inefficiency can be found, a blockchain can be used to stamp it out once and for all.

Industry

Modern business tends to run on the backs of those in a wide variety of administrative positions who do little more than manage various databases and ensure that numbers are recorded properly. Auditing firms, auditors, solicitors, supervisory boards, and most of the financial sector exist based on the need for third party verification for some type of transaction or another. As such, the biggest disruption that it will cause in this instance is the removal of a need for most of these services completely.

This improved method of verification is going to create change across a wide variety of industries as distributed ledgers offer up a chance to improve the overall level of trust in each system it is connected to. As every transaction is going to be instantly visible to everyone who is a part of it, it naturally ensures that every contract and even every payment is going to be much more trustworthy than its contemporaries that are made through more traditional systems.

This will likely result in an extreme shift of power away from those who are in charge of keeping an eye on these transactions, though this will probably not benefit new businesses as much as they might expect. Rather, it will be existing businesses who will be able to leverage their existing resources in new ways that are going to see the most benefit from this new and improved way of doing business. When done correctly, it will help to ensure that they end up in new, and more profitable, positions than they were previously in.

All told, this will serve to increase the overall rate of adoption for blockchain technology as a whole. This is due to blockchain technology being inherently social in nature. As such, the more people who use it, the more useful it becomes and so on and so forth until the technology reaches a mass saturation point where more than fifty percent of the population interacts with at least one blockchain a day.

Success in Cryptocurrency Investing

Do a mix of the above?

A mix of the above can be used to play safe when learning about and enjoying everything that cryptocurrency has to offer. In investment mode, you can have one instance of your bot; once in trade mode, you can trade a little by hand, and you can store the rest of your funds in a safe offline wallet. Perhaps, your wallet exceeds all your other good intentions, and maybe, your bots will save you from your emotional trade, but here's the thing: if one thing works well for you and the others do not, you know what kind of investor/trader you might want to concentrate on being.

Knowing the market cryptocurrencies may imitate traditional financial assets.

Still, they are undeniably exceptional, acting both as a forward-looking representation of natural products and, at the same time, as an ultimate innovation.

Cryptocurrencies are infamously unpredictable and erratic. Sometimes, inexplicable spikes in prices are typical for the crypto-investor. Such occurrences have resulted in add-ons to the crypto-sphere lexicon. HODL, a misrepresentation of hold that has become a mantra for crypto investors, is intended to ease the fears of investors as uncertainty inevitably comes in.

Bitcoin is volatile

This is the first fact you should know when investing. Bitcoins are the most commonly used cryptocurrency, and they are volatile, hence while investing, be mindful of this. The prices of Bitcoin fluctuate and plummet occasionally. There are reports of cyber hacks, and the exchange rates may not be the same throughout the year. Although the percentage fluctuation in Bitcoin price has reduced over the years, you have to be careful before making a move; study the history of the coin, and know when to take a plunge or withdraw. Investing is good, but do you know what is better than investing? Smart investing. Rule number one: Be smart with your coins.

Hold on to profits

When you start trading Bitcoins and receiving profits, it is important that you hold on to your profits for a while before selling or reinvesting. One reason why you should hold on for a while is it keeps you prepared for a viable investment that may come your way. Sometimes, people are in a hurry to sell off their coins and, thus, have an empty wallet. When a great opportunity presents itself, they are unable to buy in because they have an empty wallet. Rule number two: never have an empty wallet.

Transfers are high-speed

Unlike other financial institutions that take a lot of time, sometimes even days to complete a transaction, Bitcoin transactions do not take so long to go through. Besides the speed with which transfers can be done, there are no delays because of the absence of intermediaries, so it is just you and your network. More importantly, processing fees are not as high as other financial institutions; you have got a good deal here so start investing.

Secure your wallet

Your cryptocurrency wallet must be secure for you to generate good returns. As you already know, there are hacking attempts and scamming reports of cryptocurrencies, but if you have a secure wallet/safe, you do not have to fret over this. When you download a secure app that protects your coins, you can be sure that they will be safe from hackers. In the preceding chapter, we discussed some of the excellent apps you can rely on to secure your wallet, so benefit from them.

Buy early enough

If you want to get the best out of cryptocurrencies, you must be an early bird; this rule reigns supreme. Buy when others have not, when prices are lowest. You will be amazed at the price at which you will sell. This is one of the quickest ways to invest and make a lot of profit. If you study the market long enough, you will be able to predict when digital coins are cheap, buy them, store them in your wallet, and get ready to sell for more returns.

Profits should be higher than losses

Even if you lose money in the process of investing, your overall profit should be substantially more than your losses. It can be frustrating when you lose too much money. Hence, always weigh your profit margin and ascertain if you have made progress or have regressed.

Do not invest what you are not ready to lose

This is a vital piece of information. As much as you know of the security and user-friendliness of cryptocurrencies, it is important that you invest money that you can afford to, so do not invest money that will put you in a tight position if you end up losing them because of a bad deal. Remember that you may want to leave your coins for a while so invest money you wouldn't want to withdraw in a hurry.

Stay up-to-date

Information is key in the world of cryptocurrencies. People get into trouble when they use stale information. Cryptocurrencies are within the confines of the Internet, and a lot of changes take place quickly. You will be helping yourself considerably when you stay relevant and up-to-date. If you are not sure of something, ask questions and more importantly, read! Read material on cryptocurrencies. There is a lot of information as well as plenty of books and training available; do everything you can to be informed. Remember the saying: knowledge is power!

Diversify your portfolio

Do not put all of your eggs in one basket. Too many people get it wrong here; they place all their money in one investment, and when its returns dip, they are left with losses. You can invest in a lot of cryptocurrencies; you do not have to invest in just one. So, spread your investment by diversifying your portfolio. When you diversify, you reduce your risk level, and you have numerous avenues through which you can make a profit. It also helps you get a feel of the various platforms, which informs your decision to pull out your investment from a source or increase it.

Be rational

Investing in cryptocurrencies is an excellent move, but you must be armed with information on what to look out for before leaping. It is not about simply investing but investing properly, taking the right steps, and getting the best results. The rules shared here will help you make the right decisions. Remember this book is a definitive guide that contains all you need, so feel free to read it over again. The next chapter takes us into the future of cryptocurrencies; you will get a glimpse into what the future holds for the digital currency, and how far it can go in a world where technology is an ever-spinning wheel.

Choose the best platforms

To produce a fantastic crypto-portfolio, you need to choose the exchanges and wallet services that suit your needs.

Every product is full of its own set of complexities, but investors can, in general, value certain aspects more than others. Priority must be provided to interoperability, as well as security and functionality. If you are struggling to choose a platform, consider some of the tools and feedback that can help you select the platform that is right for you.

Be consistent

Make regular contributions to your assets that have been allocated. Cryptocurrencies can be the hottest investment class. Nevertheless, they are not a get-rich-quick scheme. Buying digital tokens like lottery tickets might help some people make sumptuous headlines. However, it will not let most investors develop a long-term investment strategy for cryptocurrencies.

Creating the ultimate portfolio on cryptocurrencies will not occur overnight. Nonetheless, when investors understand the market intricacies, diversify their assets, and use the best channels, they can continually grow these assets, which could produce the vigilant investor's high returns.

Ignore sources that are biased

When you decide to trade in cryptocurrency, it is extremely important that you do not rely on biased sources for investing ideas. The minute you start browsing online for trading options, you will come across multiple sites promising good returns. As a beginner, you should stay away from phony sites, which offer surprisingly high returns. Seek advice only from reliable sources before you begin investing. Rely on your judgment and risk appetite, and choose your portfolio accordingly. Do not get swayed by disingenuous success stories posted on certain websites and make a hasty decision.

Start small

Until you gain a good grasp on how the market works, you do not want to exhaust your life savings at once. Start small. Keep aside a small portion of your income every month for trading purposes. Invest small amounts at first, and understand the nuances of the trading process. As you start making profit, slowly increase your investments. Do not make the mistake of investing huge sums, as soon as you experience a profit for the first time. Take your time to decide the optimal portfolio for your risk appetite. Once that is figured out, you can gradually increase your investments.

Have realistic goals

Do not perceive cryptocurrency trading as an easy and quick way to become rich. As you already know, the cryptocurrency market is highly dynamic and volatile. It will take you some time to get a grasp over the trading process.

Do not try to guess and trade

Trading is not about making the right guesses. When it comes to an extremely volatile market, such as that of cryptocurrencies, it is not possible to sustain your returns purely by making guesses. You might get lucky once or twice, but your guesses can only help you to a certain extent. You need to do your homework before you make an investing decision. Even if you are not a beginner, you cannot predict exactly how the market will react tomorrow. Make sure you keep an eye on the trends, and ensure you watch out for market reports before you invest. Despite all the homework, there is still a possibility of you not making a profit. However, one failure should not deter you from doing your homework.

Be patient and do not panic

When it comes to trading with cryptocurrencies, you must learn to be patient. As a beginner, you might make some trading mistakes. Or it might take you more time to understand the nuances of the market. Do not immediately give up on trading with cryptocurrencies because of a few mistakes. In fact, you will learn more from the mistakes, which will help you make more informed decisions in the future. You must embrace the uncertain element of the future and be prepared for the worst-case scenario, too. This way, you will not panic if you make a mistake or incur a loss. You will be able to regard it as a short-term phenomenon and try to come up with a strategy to overcome this.

Learn from your mistakes

Given that the market for these cryptocurrencies is booming, it is only a matter of time and effort from your end before you make a tidy profit. Hence, you need to learn from your mistakes and correct your investing strategy accordingly. Your mistakes should be an opportunity for you to learn and better understand the market.

Plan ahead

If you want to sustain your profits from trading in the long run, you will have to come up with an investing plan. You cannot aspire to make huge profits by just focusing on trading for the day without keeping the future implications in mind.

Do not trust others completely

When it comes to trading with cryptocurrencies, you are out on your own. You cannot rely on the success stories of others alone to make your investing decisions. While you should seek the input of regular traders, you cannot blindly rely on their trading advice. This is because a certain investing strategy or choice of investments might have worked for a certain individual at that time. There is no reason for it to work that way for everyone else. Hence, you should not be basing your investment decisions solely based on what worked for others.

Pick currencies that have huge communities

With over eight hundred cryptocurrencies to date, you can be confused about which cryptocurrency you should pick. If you want to invest in something new, do not go into a currency that no one has ever heard of.

Instead, choose a currency that has a good and established platform. The currency that you choose should have the support of a lot of community members. People should know about the currency. Having a community dedicated to a particular currency would mean that the currency is popular with the people and is stable and going to last.

Do not forget to have fun!

Do not consider trading as a mundane job or activity. At the same time, do not spend too much time overanalyzing the market. This will just ruin your experience. You will forget to enjoy trading when you are overstimulated with market information. Learn to draw a line between being prudent and paranoid. When you are prudent, you will be willing to play around, have some fun, and make money on-the-go. On the other hand, if you are paranoid, you will be overthinking before making any investment decision. Time is of the essence, when it comes to trading. When the market is quickly changing, you cannot forever question your decisions and lose out on the opportunity to make money. Enjoy trading. That way, you will learn more than you expected! With time, you will be able to develop a passion for trading. When that passion sets in, it is going to be an interesting journey for you!

Now, if you are new to trading, it might be difficult for you to come up with an investing plan for the future on your own. You need to take that extra step and learn from others. Seek the advice of other experienced traders, study the market, watch out for trends, and come up with your tentative plan. When you see that your plan is working, see how you can further improve it to optimize your returns. If your plan is not working, well, it is a lesson learned! Remember, you cannot simply rely on others' counsel before investing. You need to do your bit of research as well, to validate their counsel.

7

CRYPTOCURRENCY MYTHS

Since cryptocurrencies are pretty new and many people have not had a chance to use them yet, a lot of myths have sprung up about them. People often don't understand how they work, so they are worried that the cryptocurrency may not be safe, may be a scam, or that something else may be wrong with them. This chapter will go through some of the cryptocurrency myths to give you a better understanding of how these currencies work.

"It's Not Backed By Gold or Silver—So It's No Good."

Some people are nervous about using cryptocurrencies because there is no physical material that backs it up. With traditional currencies, you have the backing of silver and gold, or the government's promise and backing. While it doesn't work this way in practice, in theory, you could take some of your money to the bank and get a certain amount of gold or silver back in the process. However, Bitcoin and the other cryptocurrencies are not designed to work this way.

Instead, these cryptocurrencies are designed through code. The code will state how much they are worth, and in many cases, only so many of each coin are available to use. For example, Bitcoin was designed with just 21 million coins available, but many of them have not been mined yet and are still not in use. This helps to keep the currency stable without needing the backing of anything else.

"Only Criminals Use It."

Yes, some criminals do work with cryptocurrencies. They like the fact that they can remain anonymous on the network and conduct their activities with a limited chance of someone being able to tell it is them. They will avoid taxes, launder money, and even sell items that are considered illegal, whether those items are illegal in their country or in the country they are sending the items to. The system is set up to help make things a bit easier for criminals to get away with these things.

But, for the most part, those who are on these networks are there because they want to use the cryptocurrency for legitimate purchases. They like all the features and the ability to make more purchases throughout the world than they were ever able to do before. And most people are doing it all legally, purchasing products that they are allowed to use in their countries and claiming the money they make in taxes. While some criminals may be on these networks, most of the people who are there are law-abiding citizens.

"A Government Agency Controls It."

We are used to working with money that has some kind of government control over it. This is the way that we have dealt with money in the past, and we know that it is backed by gold and silver and the word of our government. This is not true with Bitcoin and all of the other cryptocurrencies, although there are a few governments trying to develop their own version to use in their countries.

The fact that a government agency does not control Bitcoin and Ethereum and the other options is one of the main benefits that people enjoy when they are working with cryptocurrency. They are tired of a bank or a government agency deciding the inflation rates or how much their money's worth at the end of the day. They like the freedom of being able to earn and send money without having Big Brother there messing around with things.

"It Is a Scam."

Cryptocurrencies are brand new, and this can make them a bit scary and misunderstood by those who are not familiar with them. They are located only online with no paper counterparts for you to use. They aren't controlled by a government agency, just computer code. They allow you to remain anonymous, rather than having all your personal information stored where any hacker can get ahold of it. It can be used for purchases all around the world, without having to worry about it taking too long for the payment to go through or the high transaction fees.

All of this is stuff that we just aren't used to when it comes to our money and some people believe that it is too good to be true. But in fact, cryptocurrency is able to deliver on all its promises and more, making it the perfect choice to use. Some will still believe that it is a scam, but it is actually a safer way to make and receive payments than anything you have used in the past. And if you ever decide that you don't want to work with the cryptocurrency again, you can always exchange it for the fiat money that you want.

"Cryptocurrencies Can't Be Hacked."

This is a common misconception. **It is possible for all cryptocurrencies to be hacked.** These cryptocurrencies are designed with the help of a code, so as long as the hacker is able to get on the network and use the code how they want, it is possible for them to hack the cryptocurrency. But there are some safeguards in place that help keep the network a bit safer than what you find with traditional currencies.

First, the mining process can help to keep information about your transactions safe. The codes that go on the blockchain are set up so that if someone messes with even one number or letter in the code, it is going to mess with everything else, making it impossible to go undetected. You can also choose to work with e-wallets that provide extra protection and security to make sure that your information is not being hacked.

Sometimes, it is best if you choose to use cold storage to hold onto your currency, especially if you are not using it all that often. This allows you to keep the currency off the computer so that a hacker is not able to take it and use it how they want when you aren't around.

"Transactions in Cryptocurrency Are Untraceable."

Many people think that it is impossible to trace cryptocurrencies, but this is not true. You have ways to remain pretty anonymous on the network and keep your information safe, but the cryptocurrencies themselves can be traced. Remember that Bitcoin and the other networks want to make sure that they are transparent because this helps to build trust between them and the users, so making it impossible to trace the currency at all can make this goal hard.

All of the currencies that you use are going to be traceable. They all have histories on them, which is why some people want to switch them out to make sure transactions are not traced back to them. The ledger system with blockchain will also keep track of transactions that occur on the network, which also helps to trace the currency.

"Merchants Won't Accept Cryptocurrency."

There is a little bit of truth in this one, but it is not as bad as some people think. You may not be able to go into every traditional merchant in the country and make a purchase, but you may be surprised at how many already accept Bitcoin and other cryptocurrencies as a form of payment. Think of it like a specialty credit card, like MasterCard. Not every merchant you go to is going to accept it, but there are plenty of options that do.

When these cryptocurrencies first began, only a handful of merchants were willing to accept these currencies at all. It was a new idea that many were not that familiar with to start. But now that Bitcoin and some of the other cryptocurrencies are starting to grow, it seems like more merchants are jumping on board as well.

You can purchase items through merchants with Bitcoin in several ways. First, look through the Bitcoin (or whatever cryptocurrency you want to use) and see what merchants are available on that network. Some popular merchants already work through these networks, and you are able to make your purchases without a lot of hassle.

You can also use cryptocurrencies with a few merchants, but they aren't available online. They can use special machines that will scan your QR code in a store and take the Bitcoin out of your wallet. These are growing in popularity with some of those companies who want to reach out to the cryptocurrency crowd but who haven't found ways to be online or on the right network yet.

You will find that there are ways around the stores that don't accept cryptocurrency as a payment right now. For example, Amazon doesn't accept these kinds of currencies. but you can take your Bitcoin and other cryptocurrencies, purchase some gift cards, then use those to purchased items on Amazon. This may not be the most direct method, but it helps you to open up even more merchants to work with.

FINAL WORDS

Investing is a matter of knowledge, practice and information management, and preparation, regardless of the asset you are willing to work with.

Cryptocurrency has attracted millions of users and amateur investors around the world who are, in most cases, guided by the emotions on the market, over an asset whose value is only based on the supply and demand and generates huge gaps and instability of the price.

If you are planning to invest in cryptocurrency, make sure to get the right information, study as much as you can about how the currency behaves. Be aware of news and related material that can have an impact on its price. Getting started can be intimidating, especially if you have never been directly involved in investments or trades before. Unlike traditional currency, whereby you can hire an investment portfolio manager to do the work for you, you are responsible for investing in and trading your own cryptocurrencies.

FINAL WORDS

Fortunately, many exchange networks allow you to make this process easy, even for beginners who have little background knowledge on the trading side of finances. However, before you fully commit to any particular cryptocurrency, it is important that you take additional time to research that specific cryptocurrency. There are constantly new forms of cryptocurrencies emerging, and each one has unique traits, properties, and benefits. They also change rapidly and so can their popularity. If you want to make the best move, investigate the specific coin you are most interested in before you commit to purchasing anything.

Cryptocurrency is one way by which Bitcoin traders can avoid issues with the middlemen of business. It is a cross between assets and currencies, like the U.S dollar. As a beginner, it is advised that you do not just jump into it. Cryptocurrency, just like other investment programs, requires you to exercise a lot of discipline and risk management skills.

You also should ensure that you don't see this as a way of getting quick money. Know that the investors are becoming more knowledgeable about these things, and it's pushing them into making more calculated investment decisions!

Without a doubt, cryptocurrency is the currency of the future. Cryptocurrency offers a number of benefits, including the fact that it is based on Blockchain technology, which makes it easy to monitor, transparent, tamper-proof, and fast (in terms of transactions).

Consumers must understand how this currency is developing and whether their country supports or opposes it. Laws and the current financial structure could change overnight, bringing with them completely new modes of payment and earning.

FINAL WORDS

The main thing required of you is to believe in yourself and in the cryptocurrency market. After all, it is those people who believed in Bitcoin a few years ago that now possess huge fortunes and are influential today. Therefore, believe in the dawn of the cryptocurrency economy.

REFERENCES

Bhardwaj, A. (2017). *CryptoCurrency For Beginners* (Vol. 1). Onlinegatha.

Levin, B. (2018). Potential for Cryptocurrency to Fund Investment in Sustainable Real Assets. *Environmental Management degree Masters Project), Nicholas School of the Environment of Duke University*.

Goleman, T. (2018). *Cryptocurrency: mining, investing and trading in blockchain for beginners. How to buy cryptocurrencies (Bitcoin, Ethereum, Ripple, Litecoin or Dash) and what wallet to use. Crypto currency investment strategies*. Zen Mastery.

Guides, T. S. (2019). How to Buy Crypto ICO–The Ultimate Guide.

Tomas, P. (2017). *Cryptocurrency 101:: A Beginners Guide To Understanding Cryptocurrencies and Tow To Make Money From Trading*. Silica Lyne.

Dugan, K. (2018). *Blockchain for Beginners: Understand the Blockchain Basics and the Foundation of Bitcoin and Cryptocurrencies*. Crb Publishing.

Guides, T. S. (2019). How to Buy Cryptocurrency–The Safest Way.

Guides, T. S. (2018). Ethereum Classic Cryptocurrency Strategy, Fakeout–Shakeout Pattern.

Mahessara, R. D., & Kartawinata, B. R. (2018). Comparative Analysis of Cryptocurrency in Forms of Bitcoin, Stock, and Gold as Alternative Investment Portfolio in 2014–2017. *Jurnal Sekretaris dan Administrasi Bisnis*, 2(2), 38-51.

Hassani, H., Huang, X., & Silva, E. (2018). Big-Crypto: Big data, blockchain and cryptocurrency. *Big Data and Cognitive Computing*, 2(4), 34.

Guides, T. S. (2019). Investing in Digital Currency–5 Factors to Consider.

N'Gumah, J. (2021). Evaluating Security in Cryptocurrency Wallets.

Smutny, Z., Sulc, Z., & Lansky, J. (2021). Motivations, Barriers and Risk-Taking When Investing in Cryptocurrencies. *Mathematics*, 9(14), 1655.

hao, H., & Zhang, L. (2021). Financial literacy or investment experience: which is more influential in cryptocurrency investment?. *International Journal of Bank Marketing*.

Rahim, R. A., Ling, P. S., & Khalid, M. A. S. M. (2021). ASSESSING THE PREDICTABILITY OF CRYPTOCURRENCY PRICES. *Malaysian Management Journal, 25*, 143-168.

Wu, J., Liu, J., Zhao, Y., & Zheng, Z. (2021). Analysis of cryptocurrency transactions from a network perspective: An overview. *Journal of Network and Computer Applications*, 103139.

Printed in Great Britain
by Amazon